Rainforest Buffer Zones
Guidelines for Protected Area Managers

Jeffrey Sayer

IUCN - The World Conservation Union
Forest Conservation Programme

1991

ISBN 2-8317-0072-8

Camera-ready copy by
The Nature Conservation Bureau Ltd.,
36 Kingfisher Court, Newbury, Berkshire, UK.

Printed by Page Bros

Cover photograph: Farming on the fringe of the forest in the East Usambaras, Tanzania (Jeffrey Sayer)

IUCN - THE WORLD CONSERVATION UNION

Founded in 1948, IUCN - the World Conservation Union - is a membership organisation comprising governments, non-governmental organisations (NGOs), research institutions and conservation agencies in over 100 countries. The Union's mission is to provide leadership and promote a common approach for the world conservation movement in order to safeguard the integrity and diversity of the natural world, and to ensure that human use of natural resources is appropriate, sustainable and equitable.

Several thousand scientists and experts from all continents form part of a network supporting the work of its Commissions: threatened species, protected areas, ecology, environmental strategy and planning, environmental law, and education and communication. Its thematic programmes include forest conservation, wetlands, marine ecosystems, plants, the Sahel, Antarctica, population and natural resources, and Eastern Europe. The Union's work is also supported by 12 regional and country offices located principally in developing countries.

THE IUCN COMMISSION ON ECOLOGY

The IUCN Commission on Ecology (COE) serves as the Union's source of technical advice for translating knowledge of ecological processes into practical action for conservation, sustainable management and restoration, in particular of areas degraded by human action. The IUCN programmes on Forest Conservation, Marine Conservation and Wetlands are under the umbrella of the Commission on Ecology. Commission members serve on advisory committees and in working groups associated with these programmes.

IUCN FOREST CONSERVATION PROGRAMME

The IUCN Forest Conservation Programme (formerly the IUCN Tropical Forest Programme) coordinates and reinforces activities of the IUCN members and Secretariat which deal with forests. The Programme focuses on the conservation of species and ecological processes, and on investigating and promoting sustainable use of the resources of these forests.

The Programme includes international and national policy initiatives and strategies as well as field projects addressing selected problems in managing the world's most biologically signficant tropical forests. These selected projects put the World Conservation Strategy into action by reconciling the requirements of conservation with national development and the needs of people living in forest areas. Special emphasis is given to the development of compatible uses for buffer zones around national parks and reserves.

IUCN develops its positions and policies on the basis of the concerns and information communicated by members, trends identified by monitoring activities, and the feedback from numerous field projects. Data on species of plants and animals, and on forest sites which are important for biological and ecosystem conservation, are held by the World Conservation Monitoring Centre in Cambridge, UK.

This series of publications from the Forest Conservation Programme, in conjunction with regular meetings, enables IUCN to communicate policies and technical guidance to governments, major international institutions, development planners and conservation professionals. The Programme works closely with development assistance agencies, governments and NGOS, to ensure that conservation priorities are adequately addressed in their activities.

The Forest Conservation Programme receives generous financial support from the Government of Sweden.

CONTENTS

PREFACE

This book is not an authoritative statement of the problems of buffer zones and the solutions to them. It simply aims to present some ideas on the subject, many derived from projects in which IUCN has been involved, in a way which will provoke further thought by those people who have to make decisions about land use around protected areas in the rainforests.

The case studies have been selected to illustrate a range of situations, both in terms of ecology and geographical location. They cover projects which have been successful and also some which have not produced good results. Selected references are given for those who wish to investigate the case studies and issues in further detail.

Attempts by aid agencies to work in buffer zone situations have very often resulted in failure. In general, aid agencies have been too rigid in their methodologies, too short-term in their thinking and too intent on imposing radical change on people and institutions. The essential conclusion of this book is that every situation is unique and that flexibility and sensitivity to local conditions is fundamental to success. Buffer zone activities must be low-key, long-term and must articulate sufficiently with everything else that is going on in the area where they operate. Projects have tended to work best when an individual or a small group of people have committed themselves to dealing with the conservation problems of an area over a long period of time and have done so in a way which is sensitive to the needs and values of local people.

It would be out of keeping with the spirit of this book to present a tailor-made "blue-print" for buffer zones. Inspiration for buffer zone management must come from sensitivity to local conditions. This book can only suggest some new avenues to explore.

Jeff Sayer
Gland, 22 April 1991

ACKNOWLEDGEMENTS

This book draws heavily on Oldfield's "Buffer Zones In Tropical Moist Forests - Management Guidelines And Case Studies", published in this series in 1987. My thanks go to Sara Oldfield for her work on that volume and to the numerous people who contributed case studies and comments to it.

The present volume has benefited greatly from comments and contributions from my colleagues Jeff NcNeely, Jim Thorsell and Per Ryden at IUCN in Switzerland. Alejandro Imbach, M. S. Ranatunga, Niek Bech and others working for IUCN in the field have reviewed the text and contributed from their great knowledge of buffer zone activities in the field.

Tomas Schlichter, Juan Carlos Godoy, Enrique Lahman in Costa Rica, Mark Infield in Uganda, Mike Wells at the World Bank, Jan Wind in Indonesia and Barbara Wyckoff-Baird of WWF-US have made many helpful suggestions and have provided useful material for case studies. Individuals contributing to particular case studies are acknowledged in the text.

Roçio Jimenez of CATIE, Turrialba, Costa Rica drew the illustrations which show buffer zone situations in the Talamanca area of Costa Rica. Other illustrations were prepared by Corinne Versel in Switzerland.

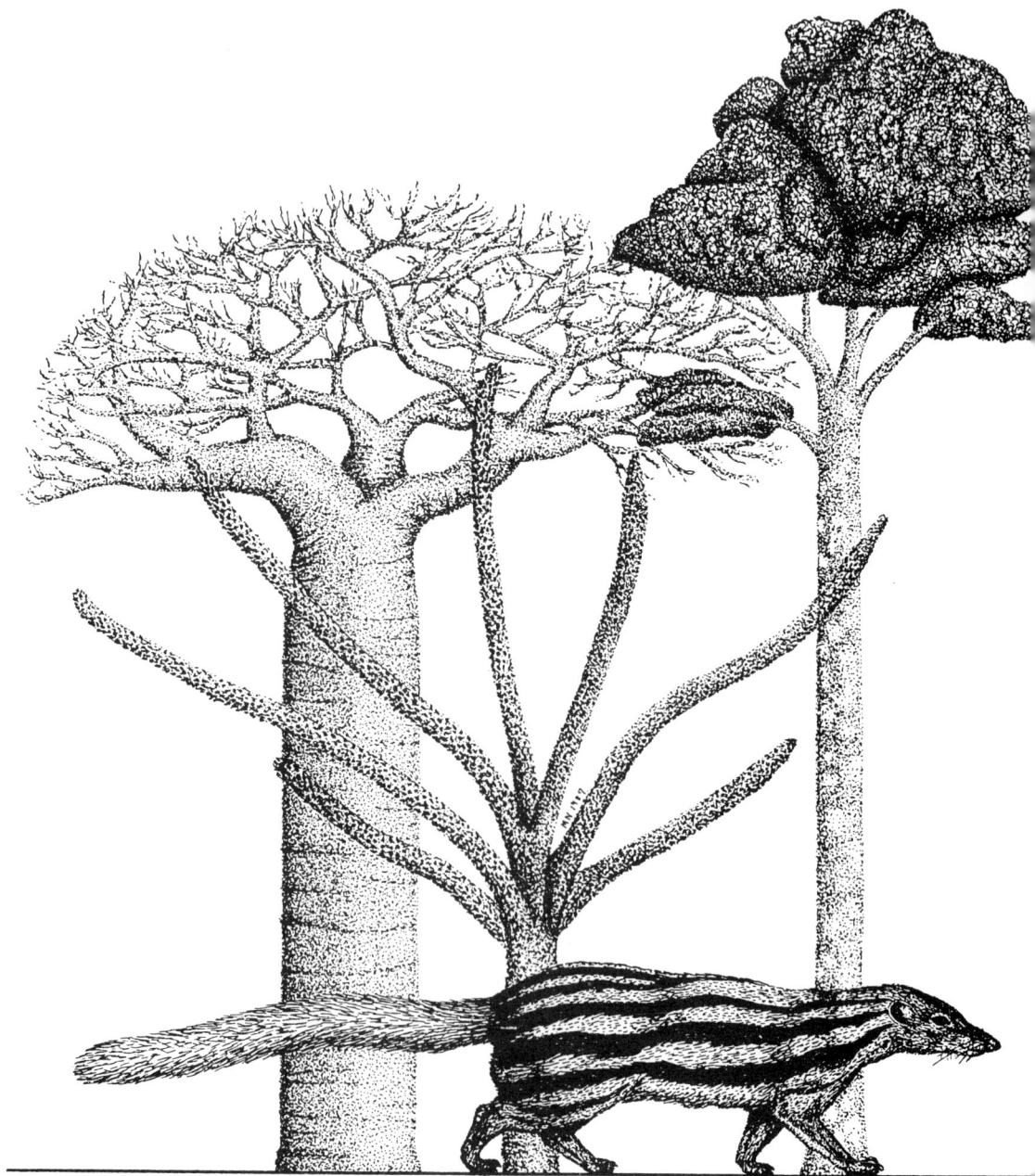

1 INTRODUCTION

This book is concerned with buffer zones in tropical closed broadleaved forests. In 1980, these forests covered an estimated 11.6 million km². Data from the World Conservation Monitoring Centre indicates that at that time about four per cent of them were located in national parks or nature reserves. Recent figures suggest that at least 10 per cent of these forests were lost in the decade from 1980 to 1990 (FAO/UNEP, 1988). During this period, however, many new parks and reserves have been established in the tropics and protected areas now cover at least six per cent of the tropical forest biome. New protected areas are still being established in Amazonia and in the Zaïre-Congo forest block. But in many parts of the tropics the human pressure on land is so great that the options for establishing new parks and reserves are rapidly disappearing. In Madagascar, West Africa and the Atlantic coastal areas of Brazil the forests are already reduced to small isolated fragments, scattered through landscapes which are predominantly agricultural.

These small island parks and reserves will not be enough to conserve all the values of tropical forests. In particular, large wide-ranging animals, and those tree species that exist at very low densities, will be very much at risk in small protected areas. Similarly, if dense human settlements exist close to the boundaries of the protected areas, there will inevitably be problems of agricultural encroachment, poaching and illegal harvesting of wood and other forest products.

Experience has shown that, in these situations, legal protection is rarely sufficient to guarantee the continuing integrity of conservation areas. Local people, often with good reason, frequently see parks as government-imposed restrictions on their legitimate rights. Patrolling by guards, demarcation of boundaries and provision of tourist facilities will therefore not deter them from agricultural encroachment. Illegal hunting and gathering of forest products will be difficult to control. Laws which are resented by the majority of the population are difficult to enforce. In these situations, protected areas lose support and credibility, and their condition rapidly deteriorates. New systems and new ideas are needed to bridge the gap between the immediate needs of local people and the long-term objectives of protected area systems.

The message that protected areas should respond to the needs of local people emerged from the Third Congress on National Parks and Protected Areas at Bali in 1982 and was reinforced by the MAB/Unesco Biosphere Reserves Action Plan adopted at Minsk, in the USSR, in 1984. In addition to these international initiatives, day-to-day realities have forced many park managers to consider the needs of local people, and most management plans now include provision for "buffer zone" activities. In reality, however, plans for activities going beyond physical and legal protection and provision of infrastructure for patrolling and tourism, have rarely been implemented. An important reason for this is that protected area managers rarely have jurisdiction over land outside the legal limits of their park or reserve. Moreover, they rarely have training in the skills which are needed to work effectively with local communities. The park manager's job is not helped by the fact that the institutions responsible for agricultural and forestry development rarely understand that land adjacent to protected areas should be treated rather differently from similar land elsewhere.

Buffer zones have been defined as "areas peripheral to national parks or reserves which have restrictions placed on their use to give an added layer of protection to the nature reserve itself and to compensate villagers for the loss of access to strict reserve areas" (MacKinnon 1981). In this book, however, the term "buffer zone" is used to cover a wide range of conservation and development activities which can be applied to the areas adjacent to parks and reserves to protect them against external pressures, and deliver benefits to local people. A basic objective is to surround protected areas with vegetation which, if not completely natural, does at least allow some animal and plant species to extend beyond the boundaries of the totally protected core. For the purposes of this book, the following working definition of a buffer zone has been adopted:

> **"A zone, peripheral to a national park or equivalent reserve, where restrictions are placed upon resource use or special development measures are undertaken to enhance the conservation value of the area."**

The concept of buffer zones is not new. In the 1950s the profits from tourist hunting around the Nsefu Game Reserve in Zambia's Luangwa Valley were used to pay for social facilities for the local communities who had traditionally hunted in the area. The Corbett National Park in northern India has long enjoyed the physical protection of managed forests of sal

Shorea robusta; the forest service harvests the timber and local people gather non-wood products in semi-natural forests which provide an extended habitat for the park's wildlife.

The idea of supporting buffer zone projects has proved very attractive to many donors of international development assistance. These organisations clearly see the need to invest in resource conservation, and many of their constituents in donor countries are happy to see aid money spent on preserving natural areas. However, for ideological reasons it is difficult for aid agencies to invest their money in "policing" activities around national parks, especially since these activities were usually aimed at limiting the activities of those poor rural people who were supposed to be the prime beneficiaries of the aid programmes. Buffer zone projects combine the two primary aims of development assistance: the wise use of resources and the increased well-being of poor rural people.

During the 1980s there has been an enormous upsurge of interest in buffer zones. This has largely been driven by the wish of people in rich countries to conserve nature in the tropics and, at the same time, contribute to improving the welfare of the people living in these countries.

Because many of these buffer zone activities were driven by outside donor support they usually took the form of "projects". They were additional to the normal activities of the management authorities of the protected areas; they were usually maintained for a limited period of time and were totally dependent on outside support, both for funding and often for technical staff. They often required expertise which fell outside the training and normal activities of the staff of protected areas, and they usually did not fit easily into the organisation of land management in the countries concerned.

Conservation organisations suddenly found a bonanza of funds available to them for buffer zone work and some were tempted to rush into ambitious development programmes. In many cases they were embarking upon activities that differed little from the integrated rural development programmes which have proved so frustrating and unproductive for the conventional aid agencies over the last two decades. There was a notable tendency to focus on *technologies* for the management of buffer zones. Different groups advocated agroforestry, tree plantations, natural forest management, sustained yield hunting and a plethora of other land uses which were considered to be ecologically well-adapted. The term "ecodevelopment" was coined and came to be applied to the sorts of activities that people perceived as being appropriate for buffer zones.

As with Integrated Rural Development in the 1960s and 70s, so the results of these buffer zone projects have been mostly disappointing (Wells *et al.*, 1990). There were few, if any, instances where outside agencies could leave in the knowledge that the conservation problems of an area were solved. Even defining projects from the concept stage to genuine achievement on the ground, has not always been easy; many projects have spent years accumulating information on their target area, and conducting negotiations with local communities, without being able to make the vital transition to practical work on the ground. But there are some buffer zone initiatives where considerable progress has been made, and much has been learned. This book is a review of some of these. It does not attempt to prescribe in detail what should be done in buffer zones; it concentrates instead on how one should approach the problems and tries to identify the basic principles which should be observed in supporting the conservation of biologically important areas. The best examples have not been short-term aid projects but initiatives taken by local community groups or resource managers who have made creative attempts to solve the day to day problems which they faced.

Further Reading

Collins, N.M., Sayer, J.A. and Whitmore, T.C. 1991. *Conservation Atlas of Tropical Rainforests: Asia and the Pacific*. McMillans, London

FAO/UNEP 1988. An interim report on the state of the world's forest resources in developing countries. FAO, Rome.

MacKinnon, J. 1981. Guidelines for the development of conservation buffer zones and enclaves. Nature Conservation Workshop PPA/WWF/FAO, Bogor, Indonesia.

MacKinnon, J. and MacKinnon, K., Child, G. and Thorsell, J. 1988. Managing protected areas in the tropics. IUCN Gland, Switzerland and Cambridge, UK.

McNeely, J.A. and Miller, K.R. (Eds) 1982. *National Parks, Conservation and Development*. Proceedings of the World Congress on National Parks. Bali, Indonesia, 11-22 October 1982. Smithsonian Institution Press.

Sayer, J.A. and Whitmore T.C. 1990. Tropical moist forests: destruction and species extinction. *Biological Conservation* **55**: 199-213.

Sayer, J.A. 1991. *Tropical Forest Conservation*. UNASYLVA, FAO, Rome, Italy.

Wells, M., Brandon, K., and Hannah, L. 1990. People and parks: Linking protected area management with local communities. (Draft MS) The World Bank, Washington, DC.

BOX 1

Benefits of Buffer Zones

Buffer zones provide gradients between totally protected land and intensively used land. As such they cannot be easily defined or allocated to categories. Every situation is unique. However the following characteristics should apply to all buffer zones:

Biological benefits
- Provide a filter or barrier against human access and illegal use of the strictly protected core zone or conservation area.
- Protect the strictly protected core zone or conservation area from invasion by exotic plant and animal species.
- Provide extra protection against storm damage, drought, erosion and other forms of damage.
- Extend the habitat and thus population size of large, wide-ranging species in the protected area.

Social benefits
- Provide a flexible mechanism for resolving conflicts between the interests of conservation and those of the inhabitants of adjacent lands.
- Compensate people for loss of access to the strictly protected core zone or conservation area.
- Improve the earning potential and quality of the environment of local people.
- Build local and regional support for conservation programmes.
- Safeguard traditional land rights and cultures of local people.
- Provide a reserve of animal and plant species for human use and for restoring species populations and ecological processes in degraded areas.

The value of buffer zones will be greater to the extent that they meet the following criteria:
- tree cover and habitats should be maintained as far as possible in a near-natural state;
- the vegetation of buffer zones should resemble that of the protected area, both in species composition and physiognomy;
- buffer zones should have similar biological diversity to the protected area;
- the capacity of the ecosystem in the buffer zone to retain and recycle soil nutrients should be retained as far as possible. Similarly, buffer zone activities should not have negative impacts on the physical structure of the soil or on its water-regulating capacity.

Exploitation of buffer zones should, as far as possible, make use of traditional, locally adapted lifestyles and resource management practices.

2 LEGAL AND INSTITUTIONAL CONSIDERATIONS

There are few countries where national legislation allows national park and reserve agencies to manage land as a buffer around protected areas. Indeed, it would often be inappropriate and unnecessary for a protected area agency to exercise exclusive management control over areas outside the protected area estate. Most would not have the competence or the resources to do this properly. There are however, legal provisions in a number of countries which allow types of land management which are consistent with the purposes of buffer zones. The two principle mechanisms are:

(i)   laws which recognise the traditional rights of local people to harvest forest products in different categories of reserves; and

(ii) laws which provide for "Extractive Reserves", that is reserves where traditional inhabitants are allowed to live, and continue to make use of various forest resources in a sustainable way, whilst maintaining the natural biodiversity of the site.

IUCN's Commission on National Parks and Protected Areas recognises four categories of protected area which could provide a legal basis for buffer zones around totally protected areas (Mackinnon *et al.*, 1986):

Category 5: *Protected landscapes*. These maintain nationally significant natural landscapes characteristic of the harmonious interaction of man and the land while providing opportunities for public enjoyment through recreation and tourism.

Category 6: *Resource reserves*. These protect the natural resources of an area for future use and prevent or contain development activities that could affect those resources. In several tropical countries forest reserves fall into this category.

Category 7: *Natural biotic area/anthropological reserves*. These allow the way of life of societies living in harmony with the environment to continue undisturbed by modern technology.

Category 8: *Multiple-use area/managed resource area*. These provide for the sustained production of water, timber, wildlife, pasture and outdoor recreation, with the conservation of nature primarily oriented to the support of these activities.

In addition, Category 4 areas (managed nature reserves and wildlife sanctuaries), together with a variety of categories of managed forest reserves, can also function as buffer zones.

Few national legislations recognise such categories of inhabited land as reserves, but where they do, they provide a strong legal base for buffer zones. Such laws make it possible to surround totally protected areas with hunting reserves, managed forests or indigenous peoples' reserves, all of which provide excellent buffer zone functions. The essential element is that no permanent change in the type of land use is permitted, and offtake of harvested products is strictly controlled.

The existence of such laws provides the ideal framework for buffer zone management and all tropical forest countries would be well advised to expand the legal basis for their protected areas systems by including such categories. However, the absence of such laws does not preclude successful development of buffer zones. In many situations it is possible to develop administrative agreements whereby protected area agencies can influence the programmes of other sectoral government agencies in areas adjoining parks and reserves. Local government authorities and national or regional planning agencies should facilitate the necessary coordination. Many of the best buffer zone initiatives have been based upon *ad hoc* arrangements between concerned local officials and populations.

Many protected areas are located in remote parts of countries, where government institutions are relatively weak. In other situations central government authorities have shown little interest in buffer zone problems. In both these circumstances some useful buffer zone initiatives have been based upon informal arrangements, often negotiated between enterprising protected area staff and their local counterparts in other government agencies. Complex legal and administrative measures have sometimes been perceived as necessary to meet the needs of aid donors. They often contribute little to solving practical problems on the ground. However, informal arrangements which work well for small-scale interventions may be less appropriate as the scale of buffer zone activities increases.

It is frequently possible to integrate conservation needs into regional planning even when formal buffer zones cannot be established. In Thailand, for example, the Rural Development for Conservation Programme is seen as a more appropriate alternative to the delineation of buffer zones (Wells *et al.*, 1990). The aims of this programme - to improve the living standards of rural communities at the same time as enhancing protection of national parks - fulfil the same objectives as buffer zones. Above all, the link between wildlife conservation and rural development should be seen as an attractive goal in all environmental and social planning in and around protected areas.

Some examples of legal measures to facilitate buffer zones are the following:

In Zaïre, the protected area authority (Institut Zaïrois pour la Conservation de la Nature) is legally empowered to regulate some human activities within 50 kilometres of the boundary of gazetted protected areas. The intention behind this was to allow law enforcement staff to more effectively restrict transport of weapons and poached animal products. It is now considered applicable for restricting other activities in areas adjacent to national parks, although it has not been widely applied for this purpose.

The legislation in Cameroon provides an alternative model for buffer zone control (IUCN, 1989). Provision is made for defining the legal limits of the buffer zone as "a protection zone situated at the periphery of each national park, nature reserve or wildlife reserve, intended to mark a transition between these areas and the areas where hunting and agriculture can be freely practised". The buffer zones are subject to the same protection as parks and reserves, except that the director of the protected area authority may authorise agriculture and habitation. This constitutes the equivalent of "reverse listing" used for species protection, whereby all species are protected except those on a "non-protected" list. The only uses that may be made of buffer zones are those specifically approved by the national park authority. Buffer zones are gazetted for some protected areas and some people live in these but application of the law to formally legitimise their presence does not appear to have occurred. Nevertheless, the Cameroon law could allow the managers of protected areas to reconcile conflicts with tradtional users of natural areas.

Several protected areas on the densely settled islands of Java and Bali in Indonesia contain inhabited enclaves. The protected area authorities have adopted the view that the only realistic way to deal with this situation is to adopted the view that the only realistic way to deal with this situation is to include these enclaves in the gazetted protected areas. These are then managed as "internal" buffer zones. This effectively means that the zonation applied to protected areas includes a variety of categories of partial reserves where the management objective is to restrict certain activities of the resident population. This approach has been viewed by many conservationists as conceding too much control to local communities. This is especially so when those communities are responsible for depleting the fauna and flora of natural areas of international importance for conservation. The situation is complicated by the fact that there are often fundamental contradictions between the traditional Indonesian "Adat Law" governing local peoples' land rights and the central government laws governing protected areas. The primacy of "Adat Law" is enshrined in the Indonesian constitution.

Some protected areas in the Ecuadorean Amazon have suffered agricultural encroachment. It is proposed that rather than de-gazette these areas, the national parks' authority should manage them as partial reserves, or buffer zones. Local people would be allowed to continue to practice agriculture and to harvest forest products, but restrictions would be applied to safeguard the natural values of the areas.

The minimum legal requirement for buffer zones is that the protected area authority should be consulted before any changes are made in the use of land adjacent to protected areas. Industrialised country laws normally require that planning procedures be observed before the use of any land is changed. Much of this planning legislation had its origins in the need to protect private landowners against the pollution and inconvenience of having industrial developments sited adjacent to their properties. Many countries have now adopted such laws to allow for restrictions to be applied to changes in the use of all land.

Protected area authorities, as landowners, can thus raise objections to changes in the use of land adjacent to their protected areas. Public Inquiries are a common requirement prior to decisions on land use changes. Environmental assessment legislation also provides safeguards against some types of land use changes but is normally applied only in the case of major industrial or infrastructure developments. Both national land use planning legislation and environmental impact assessment legislation tends to be weak in tropical developing countries and its application is often restricted to decision making on major governmental and internationally funded development projects. Protected area authorities should make greater use of this sort of legislation for controlling land use in buffer zones and, where such legislation is weak or absent, should encourage the development of appropriate legal measures.

The protected area authoritiy must be seen as a credible advocate of improved buffer zone management. This means that the protected area itself must be well managed. It must be perceived by local people and local authorities as being an important regional resource. It will help if the protected area is seen to be important; if it receives many visitors or is a location for educational activities for local children. Its staff should maintain high professional standards and the protected area infrastructure should be well maintained. It will be difficult to generate support for buffer zone initiatives around a neglected or unvisited protected area.

Guidelines

1 Various categories of partial reserves, notably multiple-use mangement reserves, provide the ideal legal framework for buffer zones. These should be located in zones surrounding totally protected areas. Provision for such reserves should be included in national legislation.

2 Planning laws and Environmental Impact Assessment laws which require consultation with the protected area authority for any change in land use around parks and reserves could provide valuable tools to strengthen control of buffer zones.

3 The absence of a defined legal basis for buffer zones need not be an obstacle to their establishment. Much can be achieved through management agreements or informal arrangements with individuals, communities and appropriate government agencies.

4 A sound legal framework for the protection and mangement of the totally protected area and effective enforcement of this legislation are essential in order to give rationale and credibility to buffer zone programmes.

5 Whereas it is clearly important that the protected area authority has an influence over land use decisions in the buffer zone, it is not essential that this authority should have operational responsibility for managing buffer zone development activities. Management authority will depend upon local circumstances and the specific competence of the agencies involved.

6 **A wide variety of institutional mechanisms can be used to manage buffer zones.** These can range from the employment of a "Community Relations Officer" by the protected area authority, to total operational control of the land by the private sector, state corporations, sectoral government agencies or the protected area authority itself.

BOX 2
Tropenbos Programme

New approaches to the conservation of tropical moist forests call for an understanding of both biological and social processes operating in the forest ecosystems. Understanding how these processes inter-relate, for example is important in designing management systems for the buffer zones of tropical forest protected areas. An international research programme called Tropenbos is coordinating the study of causes and effects of tropical deforestation, and possible remedies. The Tropenbos programme recognises that biological solutions have to fit within the social and cultural framework of the local inhabitants.

The Tropenbos programme is currently coordinating research at six locations:

- South America: Tapajos region, Brazil; Avaracuara region, Colombia
- Africa: Taï region, Côte d'Ivoire; Cristal Mountains, Gabon
- Asia: East Kalimantan, Indonesia; Kerinci National Park, Indonesia

Research Work at Taï, in the Côte d'Ivoire, includes a detailed study of the Parc National de Taï and its buffer zone, which will help to solve problems caused by recent human settlement. Land use and buffer zone management studies are also being carried out for Kerinci National Park. At all the above sites both biological and socio-economic research will be carried out to provide valuable information for sustainable utilisation of tropical forest buffer zones.

Various publications resulting from the Tropenbos research programme will be valuable for protected area managers, especially the guides and handbooks that will be particularly useful for practical management purposes.

Further Reading

Gartlan, S. 1989. *La Conservation des Écosystems Forestiers du Cameroon.* IUCN, Gland, Switzerland and Cambridge, UK.

IUCN. 1989. *La Conservation des Écosystems Forestiers en Afrique Centrale.* IUCN, Gland, Switzerland and Cambridge, UK.

MacKinnon, J. and MacKinnon, K., Child, G. and Thorsell, J. 1988. *Managing Protected Areas in the Tropics.* IUCN Gland, Switzerland and Cambridge, UK.

Wells, M., Brandon, K. and Hannah, L. 1990. People and parks: Linking protected area management with local communities. (Draft MS) The World Bank, Washington, DC.

CASE STUDY 1

Legal status of the buffer zone around the Taï National Park, Côte d'Ivoire

Côte d'Ivoire Act number 77.348 of July 3rd 1977 prohibits specified land uses in a 66,000ha *Partial Faunal Reserve* on the periphery of the Taï National Park. A Ministerial Decree in 1983 extended this "buffer zone" to about 90,000ha. Responsibility for the management of the area lies with the National Parks and Reserve Management Department, and Water and Forests Department of the Ministry of Agriculture. The law does not designate specific functions or activities for the buffer zone and in reality the area is considered an extension of the protected core area. The authorities are demarcating the protected area boundary outside the buffer zone with a 15-20m wide bulldozed strip, and no attempt is being made to develop any uses for the local population.

The problems of the Taï National Park are particularly acute. The park covers the last really extensive forest area in the Upper Guinea forest belt and protects many rare and endangered species. The region has experienced spectacular population growth in the past few decades. Baoulé and Dioula peoples from the north of the country have moved into the forest belt to grow coffee and cacao, initially with encouragement from the government. This deprived the traditional forest dwelling Guéré and Oubi peoples of their community forests and forced many of them into illegal land settlement and poaching. Forced resettlement of various peoples in response to changing "buffer zone" boundaries has built up considerable resentment amongst the local populations. At present any encroachment on even the buffer zone is perceived by the authorities, and by some international conservation organisations, as a direct threat to the integrity of the protected area.

The Dutch sponsored *Tropenbos* programme now proposes to investigate a variety of sustainable ways of using timber and non-wood products from the buffer zone and other surrounding forest areas. The programme will be developed in close collaboration with local communities and will contribute to developing acceptance of the national park amongst the people.

Source: Vooren, A.P. (in press). Appropriate buffer zone management strategies for the Taï National Park, Côte d'Ivoire. Actes de l'atelier sur l'aménagement et la conservation de l'écosystème forestier tropical humide. Guyane Francaise, Mai 1990, Unesco, Paris.

CASE STUDY 2

Institutional arrangements for the Yaxja-Nakum-Naranjo Project in northeastern Peten, Guatemala

Yaxja, Nakum and Naranjo are major Maya ruins located in the forests of the northeastern Peten, Guatemala. The forests are threatened by the advance of agricultural colonists from the south, who are clearing the forest. The area falls within the 1 million hectare Maya Biosphere Reserve which was declared in 1990 to protect the natural and cultural values of the region. The National Commission for the Environment and IUCN collaborated in the preparation of a "Strategy for the sustainable development of the region", which identified stabilisation of the agricultural frontier zone around Yaxja, Nakum and Naranjo as a priority.

The project began in 1989 and consisted only of a coordinator with a vehicle and office. The coordinator lived in the area and had the mandate to facilitate the interactions between the various agencies who influenced land management. The principal partners were the National Commission for Protected Areas (CONAP), Guatemala Institute of Archaeology and History (IDAEH), The Guatemala Planning Secretariat (SEGEPLAN), the National Commission for the Environment (CONAMA) and the Peten Regional Development Council. The first four months were spent in getting to know these various institutions and making contact with local communities. A team including specialists from the social sciences, agronomy, forestry and conservation was then sent in to develop a set of activities for the following year. These activities included support to local community organisations and detailed assessment of the areas where the project would focus its attention. A steering committee and coordinating commission were established.

No single institution will have exclusive responsibility for the buffer zone. The objective is to influence the programmes of all institutions active in the area so that they are consistent with conservation objectives. The project is still in its infancy but the response has so far been favourable, and it appears probable that the multi-institution approach to buffer zone management will prove the most effective formula for the Peten.

References: Garrett, K. and Garrett, W.E. 1989. La Ruta Maya. *National Geographic* **176**(4).
Schwarz, N. 1991. *Forest Society*. University of Pennsylvania Press, Philadelphia, PA.

CASE STUDY 3

Gandoco Manzanilla and Barro de Colorado Wildlife Sanctuaries in Costa Rica

Wildlife reserves under Costa Rican law are conservation areas where private land ownership is possible. The law restricts changes in land use but people are allowed to pursue their traditional activities. As part of its support for the establishment of the Gandoco Manzanilla Wildlife Reserve the local NGO ANAI (see case study 14) helped the residents of the area to register their title to the land. ANAI also supported local development activities by these people which would be consistent with conservation objectives. The underlying philosophy was that land owners would be the best stewards of land resources. The intentions may have been too complicated for the local situation, or they may simply have been misunderstood. People were happy to receive title to the land, but were reluctant to accept the restrictions on its subsequent use. This has resulted in some local opposition to the establishment of the reserve.

A similar situation is now emerging in the Barro de Colorado Wildlife Reserve further north along the Caribbean coast. The area is of outstanding biological value but the presence of a significant human population means that it cannot be gazetted as a national park. An attempt is being made to manage the area as a wildlife reserve, with parts of it under private ownership. This is running into similar problems to those at Gandoco Manzanilla. There is considerable local opposition to the imposition of restrictions on use of the private land and an NGO (The League against Barro de Colorado) has been formed to fight the reserve.

These examples highlight the danger of trying to manage important conservation areas under local, private ownership. People may readily accept the principle of restrictions on use in order to get title to land. However, in the longer term, and especially as new land use options become available to them, it will be very difficult to enforce land use-change restrictions. This problem will occur in privately owned buffer zones and is potentially a series flaw in the concept of "indigenous" and "extractive" reserves.

Source: Wells, M., Brandon, K., and Hannah, L. 1990. People and parks: Linking protected area management with local communities. (Draft MS) The World Bank, Washington, DC.

15

Agathis macrophylla (Corinne Versel, 1989)

16

3 LAND TENURE

The ownership of land will obviously be a major influence in determining the nature of buffer zones. Where the land is state-owned, it may be relatively easy to gazette reserves or impose restrictions on use. The setting aside of communally-owned or private land for buffer zones will involve more complex negotiation and will raise the issue of compensation. National land tenure laws are often inconsistent with traditional systems of communal ownership of land and its resources. In these situations it may be difficult to obtain local acceptance and support for legal gazettement measures. Traditional *adat* law guarantees access to traditionally-used lands for forest dwelling populations in Indonesia and effectively precludes legal reservation of land for conservation in many areas.

The issue of land tenure in influencing the management of tropical forests is exceedingly complex. In industrialised countries legislation has evolved to reconcile the interests of individuals, communities and the state. In many tropical countries there are serious flaws in land tenure laws. This sometimes results from the maintenance of rather simple laws enacted under colonial administrations which place excessive control in the hands of government authorities. There are many countries where official "government" laws are inconsistent with traditional practices and where actual practice is a compromise worked out at the local level amongst the government authorities, local communities and individuals.

In the face of such complexity it is difficult to draw broadly applicable conclusions in a book of this sort; persons concerned with buffer zone management must ensure that they fully understand the traditional and actual legal land tenure situation. Practice may prove to be based upon elements of both history and the application of modern law. Any attempts to modify the land tenure situation should be based upon two principles:

- land rights of local people should take precedence over those of distant resource users;

- laws should guarantee access to forest resources for forest people whilst placing restrictions upon over-exploitation of these resources or clearance of the land.

17

In areas where populations are dense or increasing rapidly, or where shifting agriculture is encroaching upon protected areas, it may be helpful to award secure individual land tenure to farmers in buffer zones. This will encourage them to invest in intensification of their agriculture and will make them more likely to introduce trees to their farming systems.

In many countries it is still possible to acquire title to public forest land by clearing it. This is especially so in countries where settlement of forest areas is officially seen as desirable or necessary. The sort of uncontrolled settlement that this tends to provoke is clearly undesirable in land peripheral to forest areas allocated for conservation. Legislation to deny such rights in specified buffer zones would normally be necessary. Rights to use land in certain ways and to collect specified resources will usually be more easily accommodated than rights to claim ownership of the land. Several industrialised countries, for example, have legislation which allows people to own and use forest land but not to clear it. Costa Rica law allows ownership but not conversion of forest. Such legal measures to encourage maintenance of forest cover on private land are potentially powerful instruments for safeguarding buffer zones and should be adopted in other tropical countries.

The rights of tribal and indigenous peoples to the ownership of their traditional lands are recognised in international agreements, most specifically in Article 11 of Convention No. 107 of the International Labour Organization. In many countries these rights may be expressly guaranteed in national constitutions and domestic legislation.

The establishment of extractive reserves for areas inhabited by non-indigenous communities practising sustainable systems of forest use, such as tapping wild rubber and gathering brazil nuts is now being promoted in the Brazilian Amazon. This old tradition is often seen as a highly innovative approach to the conservation of tropical forests. Moreover, as a land mangement system, it bears a close resemblance to the systems applied for the management of the "commons" of parts of Europe in the Middle Ages. Specified persons, or groups of persons, held rights to certain specified products and uses of common land, but did not have exclusive rights to the land or the right to change its use. Title to the land remained with the state. An interesting account of how the system worked in medieval England is given in Tubbs (1986) who describes how the system operated in the New Forest. Collective titling of land for peasant cooperatives has been applied the conservation problems which confront us today, both in tropical forests and elsewhere, result from the breakdown of the traditional systems of managing "common land". This is the so-called "tragedy of the commons".

Guidelines

7   Buffer zones can be managed effectively if title to the land is vested in the state. The land can then be placed under a uniform mangement regime (for forestry, hunting, non-timber products etc). Sustainable extractive use by local communities can be the subject of management agreements.

8   When smallholder farmers are already using land close to protected area boundaries it is usually desirable that they should be given secure title to this land. This will encourage them to invest in agricultural intensification and perennial crops and will make it more difficult for new colonists to move into the area.

9   Land laws should favour the retention of forest on privately held land. They should never make clearance a prerequisite for tenure.

10 A balance has to be sought between ensuring secure access to forest resources for forest-dwelling people and providing control to prevent over-exploitation of these resources. Even within indigenous communities there is some stratification of society and conflicts will occur between the more entrepreneurial individuals and the more conservative. Community tenure of land is difficult to operate in rapidly evolving societies with weak institutions.

Further Reading
Bromley, D.W. and Cernea, M.W. 1989. *The Management of Common Property Natural Resources*. World Bank Discussion Paper No. 57. The World Bank, Washington, DC.
Poore, D. and Sayer, J.A. 1991. *The Management of Tropical Moist Forest Lands*. 2nd Edition. IUCN, Gland, Switzerland and Cambridge, UK.
Tubbs, C.R. 1986. *The New Forest*. Collins, London.

4 RURAL DEVELOPMENT IN BUFFER ZONES

The most endangered tropical forest protected areas are those located in areas with high human population densities, particularly where unsatisfied demand for agricultural land is forcing poor rural people to encroach upon forests. In areas where soils are poor this encroachment may take the form of unsustainable shifting cultivation which leaves behind it a degraded landscape where both conservation and agricultural values are diminished. Agricultural encroachment into forest protected areas is a major threat to the conservation of biological diversity in areas ranging from the Atlantic Coastal Forests of Brazil, much of Central America, coastal West Africa, the highlands of Eastern Africa, Madagascar and much of mainland and parts of insular Southeast Asia. In all these regions protected areas are islands in the midst of landscapes which are dominated by agriculture.

Conventional conservation measures based upon strict application of conservation laws have been difficult to apply in these situations. Laws are often perceived as being inimical to the interests of local people and their application is resented by large sectors of the population. Enforcement of conservation laws often receives little support from government authorities outside the forestry or protected area agencies and has not attracted much support from aid agencies. National conservation programmes have been starved of funds.

The saving of these forest islands, threatened by a sea of humanity, is the major challenge facing many conservation organisations in the tropics. At a time when the industrialised world is preoccupied with the problems of the rampant poverty in the tropical developing world, it is ideologically attractive to hope that the problems of the conservation of these areas can be solved, not by law enforcement, but by applying development assistance to solving the problems of small farmers, thus eliminating their need to encroach on the forest. It is in these situations that the conservation community is facing the practical test of resolving the apparently conflicting interests of conservation and development.

The ecological devastation which has been caused by many large-scale development projects is now being exposed. The public in the aid donor countries requires that its development assistance money be spent on conserving resources and not on destroying them. There is therefore a wave of interest amongst the donor agencies in supporting small-scale, ecologically sensitive development projects. When these are located adjacent to protected areas they should help to resolve conflicts between the interests of farmers and conservation. For these reasons many aid agences are now channelling money through non-governmental organisations to buffer zone projects around ecologically sensitive areas.

This has resulted in many conservation organisations involving themselves in rural development projects for the first time. The results have on the whole been disappointing; many conservation NGOs are now learning what the official development agencies knew ten years ago: that integrated rural development is conceptually fine, but it is extremely difficult to bring it about in practice.

Many of these "buffer zone" projects are operating in areas where the human population is increasing rapidly. The poverty of soils often makes it technically very difficult to achieve sustainable and productive agriculture. Societies at the agricultural frontier have weak institutions: farmers are more concerned for their own needs than for those of the community and everybody is more preoccupied with local needs than with conservation objectives established in distant cities. The problems of bringing assistance to these marginal communities has been compounded by the repeated economic crises that have afflicted third world governments, limiting their ability to sustain basic infrastructure and services. World prices of the cash crops that grow in the humid tropics, and which could have helped small farmers to move out of the subsistence economy, have plummeted.

BOX 3

Biosphere Reserves

Biosphere reserves are internationally important protected areas recognised under the Unesco Man and Biosphere Programme (MAB). The areas are chosen and managed as natural or largely undisturbed representative examples of the world's major ecosystem types. They are also selected to demonstrate the relationship between conservation and development.

Biosphere reserves ideally consist of a strictly protected core zone of the relatively intact natural vegetation with a surrounding buffer area. The core areas are often located in centres of endemism (or genetic richness) or in areas with unique natural features of exceptional scientific interest. The buffer zone is an area suitable for sustainable development. It will typically contain examples of harmonious landscapes resulting from traditional land-use patterns, and examples of modified or degraded ecosystems suitable for restoration. A variety of agricultural activities, settlements and other uses are encouraged in the buffer zones, and these are managed in ways compatible with conservation.

In most countries "Biosphere Reserves" are not categories of protected area. Rather, the term represents a concept of integrated management where conservation interests are addressed by the application of the principles contained in this book to any existing protected area and its surrounding lands. Inclusion on the Unesco list gives international recognition to the site and makes it eligible for financial support from Unesco.

The list of tropical moist forest biosphere reserves given in table 1 is not exhaustive, in that some reserves with mixed vegetation are not included.

Further Reading

Unesco/UNEP. 1984. *Conservation, Science and Society*. Contributions to the first International Biosphere Reserve Congress, Minsk. 2 Volumes. Unesco, Paris.

Table 1: Tropical Moist Forest Biosphere Reserves

Country	Reserve	Total area (ha)	Major land user	Buffer zone (ha)
Bolivia	Pilon-Lajas	100,000	Human settlement	None
Cameroon	Réserve Forestière et de Faune du Dja	500,000	None	None
Central African Rep	Basse-Lobaye Forest	18,200	Human settlement	None
China	Dinghu Nature Reserve	1,200	Tourism	950
Congo	Odzala National Park	111,000	None	None
Gabon	Reserve naturelle d'intégrale 'Ipassa-Makokou	15,000	Human settlement	5,000
Ghana	Bia National Park	7,770	None	22,800
Guinea	Mount Nimba	17,130	Engineering works	7,130
	Ziama Massif	116,170	Human settlement Forestry, Agriculture	56,170
Côte d'Ivoire	Taï National Park	330,000	None	90,000
Indonesia	Gunung Gede-Pangrango	14,000	None	Proposed
	Lore Lindu	231,000	Settlement	Proposed
	Tanjung Puting	205,000	Logging, Agriculture	None
	Gunung Leuser	946,000	Settlement	Proposed
	Siberut	56,000	Logging	Proposed

Protected area agencies have rarely had the expertise or the mandate to run rural development projects. Agriculture departments were not always present, or willing to get involved. Conservation NGOs often found it easier to deal directly with the local people and "by-pass" the government rural development structures. Where support could be sustained over a long period "by-pass" did not constitute a problem. But free-standing projects could often not sustain themselves when fixed-term donor support ended.

To satisfy the requirements of aid agency donors, many NGOs developed very detailed plans for buffer zones in which they prescribed the sorts of activities that the aid agencies were likely to find attractive. There was a period when "agroforestry" was seen as the answer to all buffer zone problems. These detailed blue-prints for buffer zone projects often failed to take account of local environmental, social or marketing constraints and resulted in the investment of money in activities which were inappropriate for the locality. Projects frequently failed to take advantage of the enormous value of the local knowledge held by rural communities; they frequently pursued objectives which were inconsistent with the aspirations of the very people whom they were trying to help. There was a tendency for projects to provide subsidies or pay salaries to people in order to meet project targets. Technology was often introduced which was far too costly for local communities to purchase or maintain. And often projects simply underestimated the time that it takes to bring about change in peoples' farming practices. Subsistence farmers in the tropics have learned by bitter experience to be extremely cautious about attempting any sort of change, they are very conservative people who, after all, can ill afford any experimental failures.

However, there are many conservation organisations that have made long-term commitments to protected areas in the tropics and have succeeded in raising the money to provide sustained support. They have often developed close working relationships with the staff of the protected area and with the communities living in the surroundings. Good projects are often those where researchers have developed a strong personal commitment to an area and have been able to generate sufficient resources to respond to urgent needs both of the protection staff and of local communities. Some of these projects have existed on very meagre resources and have been obliged to build gradually upon local initiatives and depend heavily on local knowledge and technologies. Their impacts have been less dramatic but more relevant and sustainable than those of main-stream buffer zone projects that have attempted to bring about more radical changes more rapidly.

Guidelines

11 Preoccupation with buffer zone issues should not divert attention away from the need for effective conservation management of the strictly protected core zone or conservation area and especially for rigorous enforcement of protection laws. But laws must appear useful and rational to local people, otherwise they will be very difficult to enforce.

12 Buffer zone projects should start small and be based upon both knowledge of the resources of the area and of the development needs of the people. Acquisition of this knowledge must continue throughout the life of a project and will be particularly intense during the first years.

13 Buffer zone development projects should not normally be started unless there is a reasonable probability that support will be maintained for ten to fifteen years. Buffer zone problems are rarely amenable to solutions attainable within the three to five year time spans of conventional aid projects.

14 It is neither necessary nor desirable to prepare detailed technical plans for buffer zone projects. It is more important to concentrate on putting into place a mechanism for delivering assistance in ways that are ecologically sensitive and that emerge from a careful appraisal of development possibilities and needs. This appraisal must be based on an intense dialogue with local communities. Blue-print projects, with rigid objectives, will frequently prove to be irrelevant and by tending to disrupt local institutions and practices, may be counterproductive.

15 The process of managing the dialogue with local people is of fundamental importance and requires technical expertise and resources. It cannot be achieved by visiting experts simply talking to local people. Dialogue is a two-way process and the project must contribute expertise not available to the communities; this must include improved agricultural techniques, knowledge of outside markets and an appreciation of the macro-economic environment.

16 Dialogue must be linked to practical action on the ground. Village meetings will always generate expressions of good intent but unless

incentives exist these will not necessarily be translated into changes in farming methods or in attitudes towards community managed resources.

17   Projects should not "by-pass" existing government rural development agencies, even if these appear to be inefficient. By-passing these structures diminishes the sustainability of projects and weakens the efforts of government agencies in other locations.

18   Many buffer zone projects involve paying farmers to undertake development work. They also frequently pay salary supplements to government officers to compensate them for the additional work that the project requires of them. These payments will not be sustained when outside support for the project is eventually withdrawn and they disrupt the normal functioning of government agencies. However, the conservation importance of some areas may be so great, and the probability of continuing outside support so high, that such payments may be justified.

19   Rural development activities in buffer zones should use simple technologies and local materials, and should use local labour intensively. Expensive technologies, or those requiring outside operation or maintenance should be avoided. Even excessive dependence on vehicles may undermine long-term sustainability.

20   The establishment of foundations, trusts or local non-governmental organisations can be an effective way of attracting and sustaining outside support for buffer zone programmes. These should be independent legal entities. They can hire their own staff at competitive rates, enjoy tax exempt status and have access to international funding support. They may also generate income from protected area entrance and guiding fees, sales of information materials and buffer zone products.

Further reading

Van Orsdol, K.G. 1988. *Buffer Zone Agroforestry in Tropical Forest Regions.* Forestry Support Programme, USDA Forest Services, Washington, DC.

CASE STUDY 4

Forest conservation and agricultural development in the East Usambara Mountains, Tanzania

The East Usambara mountains are located in northeast Tanzania. The remnant forest areas on the mountains have a high level of endemic fauna and flora; they are seriously threatened by illegal timber harvesting and agricultural encroachment by a dense rural population living around the forest zone. Workers brought into the area to work on tea estates have tended to abandon estate work and engage in shifting agriculture or cultivate cardamom in the forest. The problem has been aggravated by the depressed condition of the tea estates following government control of wage levels.

Cardamom cultivation presents a particular conservation problem because it is practiced under the canopy of the forest and it effectively prevents regeneration of trees. Cardamom yields decline after about eight years of cultivation and farmers then open the canopy further to obtain crops of sugar cane and manioc.

An IUCN project in the area has the objective of "...improving the villager's living conditions and the regional resource functions, while adequately preserving the forests' biological diversity and environmental value". The project is executed by the Ministry of Agriculture and Livestock Development, in collaboration with the Forestry and Beekeeping Division of the Ministry of Lands and Natural Resources. The technical staff are seconded from these ministries and there are two expatriate advisers, a forester and an agronomist.

The project has provided equipment and funding to help the local forest guards carry out their law enforcement function more effectively. It has provided materials and technical support to establish tree nurseries and plant strips of trees to demarcate forest reserve boundaries. Most of the vulnerable boundaries have now been planted with two to four rows of teak or *Eucalyptus*. Attempts to encourage villagers to establish woodlots by providing seedlings have not met with much popular support but individual farmers have been quick to take opportunities to obtain seedlings of a variety of trees to plant on their own land. Cloves and coffee have been especially successful but some multi-purpose agroforestry species have also been used.

27

Pit-sawing of valuable timber trees in the forest reserves by people from outside the area has been a major problem. Some attempt has been made to bring this under the management of communities living adjacent to the forests but the latter have no tradition of pit-sawing and have preferred to sub-contract the work to outsiders. In the long term it is intended to exploit pit-sawn timber and invest the proceeds in replanting the forest or in social facilities in the villages. The problems of managing the programmes are considerable and it is proving so difficult to limit the volume of pit-sawing that a temporary ban on all pit-sawing has had to be imposed.

Rural development activities are managed through a system of village coordinators. These are local people with intermediate-level schooling who are employed by the Regional Development Authority. One village coordinator is assigned to, and lives in, each of the 13 villages covered by the project. Seven of them are women. They are sent on short courses at government agricultural training institutions and also receive in-service training from the project staff.

The village coordinators form development committees within their villages to determine village priorities. They are the channel by which the project provides small scale support to village initiatives. This includes provision of nursery materials, seedlings and seeds, help in constructing fish-ponds and establishing contour terraces and seeds and advice for vegetable gardening.

The village coordinators meet once a month to discuss activities in their village with the project staff and the other coordinators. New ideas are disseminated through these meetings. Decisions are made collectively on the future direction of the project and the meetings also provide a form of internal evaluation for the activities at the level of each village and for the project as a whole.

The project operates in Amani Division. In 1988, this Division had a population of 23,946 people living in an area of 316km^2, a density of 75 persons per km^2. There is 10,340ha of forest reserve and 18,380ha of public land in the Division. Some of the latter is forested. There are 2,880ha of tea estates. The project has spent about US$1 million in foreign exchange, mainly for vehicles and technical advisers and has had a local currency operating budget of about US$100,000 equivalent per year.

Amongst its major physical achievements the project has planted about 500,000 trees, including 100km of boundary strips around forest reserves and 30ha of communal plantations. Five central and 168 village tree nurseries have been established. The project has also put in contour strips on 1,000 farms over an average of one to two hectares per farm and constructed 40 fish ponds.

Major attitudinal changes have included widespread adoption of contour terracing and moderate scale planting of cloves, pepper and coffee.

The project was originally intended to have a duration of ten to fifteen years. Much of the three-year first phase was taken-up with establishing the project on the ground, obtaining equipment and constructing houses.

Principal conclusions of the first phase of the Usambaras Project

- The short period of the funding commitment has made long-term planning difficult and has created insecurity among project staff.

- When the project was in its early stages with few staff and a low level of activity it operated efficiently with an informal management structure. Now that it has grown it requires more structured management and clearer lines of communication to the government ministries involved.

- Even at the level of these very small and seemingly integrated communities, cooperative ventures have not worked. Individual ownership is essential otherwise people misappropriate village-owned fish, tree seedlings, fruit and other resources.

- Changes in local community attitudes and behaviour take a long time to achieve. Effective development work only began mid-way through the first phase, the earlier period was needed to establish a meaningful dialogue with the communities and the authorities.

- Attempts to plan rural development activities in advance of the project were not very useful. Successful new ideas have all emerged from discussions and experimental plots.

- Salary supplements to government employees were essential to achieving progress on the project. A formal mechanism is needed to negotiate these. They must be consistent with similar payments made on other government projects.

- The village-coordinator system was the single biggest success of the project. It made a major contribution to raising awareness of conservation issues and has built a foundation upon which more ambitious development work can be achieved in the future.

- The ability of the project to provide small-scale assistance, rapidly and in a flexible way, to the villages has done much to build confidence and acceptance of the project. Complementary activities like football matches and film shows were valuable for this purpose.

- Communal tree planting was slow and inefficient. Results were patchy. Boundary planting was best achieved by paid labour. However, the government officially promotes communal tree planting and it has had value in raising awareness and building political support for the project.

- Law enforcement is much more efficient as a result of the project and is much better tolerated by the communities. The village coordinators have helped achieve acceptance of law enforcement.

Sources: Hamilton, A.C. and Bensted-Smith, R. 1989. *Forest Conservation in the East Usambara Mountains, Tanzania.* IUCN Tropical Forest Programme, IUCN, Gland, Switzerland and Cambridge, UK.
IUCN project staff.

CASE STUDY 5

The 'Support Zone' in the Cross River National Park Project, Nigeria

The Cross River National Park (CRNP) Project encompasses the design, establishment and development of a new moist-forest conservation area in southeast Nigeria. The park lies in two administrative divisions: about 280,000ha in Oban, and about 92,000ha in Okwango. They lie about four kilometres apart on either side of the Cross River. The project began in late 1988 with a feasibility study for the Oban Division by WWF, on behalf of the Nigerian authorities and the Commission of the European Communities. In early 1990, the study was extended to the Okwango Division, and a seven-year work programme and budget was devised.

The project design includes the boundaries and management zones of the park itself, the provision of certain kinds of rural development inputs to villages bordering the park, and the infrastructure, equipment, staff and expertise needed to implement the recommendations. There are about 76,000 people living close to the park, and partly dependent on it for income and subsistence from hunting, fishing and collecting forest produce. They live by shifting agriculture and will destroy the biological integrity of the park area within a few years unless radical changes in land use occur: this is the central problem which the project is seeking to address.

Target villages and their farmlands and communal forests are defined as a 'Support Zone', within which incentives and disincentives will be applied to encourage local people to participate actively in the protection and development of the park, and to change their land use practices to more sustainable, agroforestry-based systems. Being defined in terms of villages rather than a discrete area, the Support Zone cannot be shown on a map. Indeed, the component villages are graded according to their degree of dependence on the park and the threat they represent to it, and this will affect the level of assistance provided to each. The term Support Zone was chosen instead of buffer zone to imply a mutually supportive relationship between the park and people, rather than a defensive posture of the park against the people. This frees the term buffer zone for more appropriate use, for example where sympathetic management of adjacent forest reserves can create a transition region of partly protected habitat.

The incentive system employed by the CRNP Project is known as the Support Zone Development Programme (SZDP). It will administer directed credit, advice, grants, planting materials and other benefits to the villages on condition that the boundaries of the park are respected by the beneficiaries. The latter will register with the SZDP once it starts, and only local inhabitants will be eligible for benefits. Fraudulent registration of non-local inhabitants by village councils would dilute the fixed sum of available benefits, this should discourage the practice and also reduce immigration to the area.

In addition to the usual enforcement measures employed by the park management service, sanctions available to the CRNP Project in the event of non-compliance by Support Zone villages include: reduction or suspension of regular grant allocations, suspension of SZDP registration, refusal of loans to individuals, and withdrawal of specific privileges of certain villages to make use of parts of the park for traditional economic activities. The SZDP and the Park Management Service will thus work closely together to monitor village behaviour, and to administer appropriate 'rewards' and 'punishments'. The rewards should engender significant and sustainable economic improvements by the villages concerned, while the punishments will mostly serve to retard such progress. To establish clearly the direct link between the two options, a local Village Liaison Officer will be employed in each village to maintain communication between the village and the CRNP Project authorities.

Sources: Caldecott, J.O., Bennett, J.G. and Ruitenbeek, H.J. 1989. Cross River National Park, Oban Division: Plan for developing the Park and its support zone. Report to World Wide Fund for Nature, Godalming, UK.
Caldecott, J.O., Oates, J.F. and Ruitenbeek, H.J. 1990. Cross River National Park, Okwango Division: Plan for developing the Park and its support zone. Report to World Wide Fund for Nature, Godalming, UK.

CASE STUDY 6

Shifting agriculture and rainforest management in northeast India

Shifting agriculture, known locally as "jhum", is the main land use in the tropical forest areas of the hill regions in northeast India. The jhum system is a highly complex form of land use, involving up to 35 crop species. Pig husbandry, based on crop residues and grazing, is an integral part of the system.

Jhum is extremely energy-efficient and also allows for recycling of soil nutrient resources. Increasing population pressure has, however, led to shortening of the fallow phase in the system which, in turn, is leading to "desertification" of the landscape, despite high rainfall. Research on the jhum system has shown that a ten year cycle is the minimum length for jhum to function successfully, both ecologically and economically. This time span allows for secondary forest succession to build up soil fertility lost through forest clearance. It also helps in weed control; after about five years of secondary succession weeds are suppressed by larger shrubs and trees.

The situation in northeast India exemplifies that found around protected areas in many high rainfall tropical areas. The solution to buffer zone problems has to be sought in the broader context of efforts to stabilise shifting agriculture. In general it has proved extremely difficult to do this.

Alternative land use strategies have failed to provide a satisfactory replacement for jhum. Valley cultivation, although a successful alternative, is limited by topography. Terracing has led to increased leaching of the fragile soils and total degradation of the land after six to eight years of continuous cropping. High inputs of expensive organic fertilisers and herbicides would be necessary to maintain terrace cultivation and these are prohibitively expensive. Additionally, social considerations do not favour terracing, as the land is held under communal tenure rather than by individuals.

Generally, development strategies for tribal people of tropical northeast India have failed because they have been based on value systems imposed from outside. Development strategies must be based on an understanding of the traditional ecological and social systems. Research on the agricultural practices of northeast

India has led to the following recommendations for development:

●   Development of valley cultivation, where appropriate, using improved crop varieties.

●   Development of a plantation/horticultural economy on a cooperative basis.

●   Improvement of jhum by adding new species and varying species composition in the crop mixture.

●   Strengthening of agroforestry and ecological principles in the jhum system, for example by introducing nitrogen-fixing trees, such as *Alnus nepalensis*, and shrubs and planting a shelter belt of forest and fruit trees along the jhum plot boundary.

●   Development of animal husbandry, particularly for pigs and poultry, to supply protein needs and a source of income.

●   Promotion of more efficient energy use, by introducing improved cooking stoves and biogas technology.

Source: P.S. Ramakrishnan, School of Environmental Sciences, Jawaharlal Nehru University, New Delhi, India.

CASE STUDY 7

The Heroes y Martires de Veracruz Project: stabilising land use in the Maribios Range, Nicaragua

The Maribios Range runs along the Pacific coast of northwestern Nicaragua. The area has volcanic soils and a seasonal climate. Much of the flatter low-lying land, which is intensively used for cotton cultivation, has become concentrated in the hands of a few people who can afford mechanisation and heavy investments in agricultural chemicals. Many poorer peasants have moved into the forested uplands where they practice shifting agriculture. After the 1979 revolution the peasants were organised into cooperatives and many were given land title. But by this time most of the forest cover had gone, soil erosion was widespread and rivers and creeks were reduced to dry gullies that only contained water for a few hours after a rain storm. Pressure on the little remaining forest in the upper part of the range was high, exacerbated by seasonal fires set in pasture lands.

In 1986 IUCN began collaboration with the Natural Resources Directorate (DIRENA) to establish the Maribios Reserve and to restore the ecological balance in pilot areas around the small remaining forest patches.

The first phase worked with seven peasant cooperatives on the slopes of the Casita Volcano. The situation was studied in each cooperative and a work programme developed by the cooperative members. Each cooperative adopted different priorities. Attention focused on contouring crops, terracing, tree planting along fences and windbreaks and the construction of small stone dams in erosion gullies.

In following years the cooperatives adopted fruit plantations, restored abandoned coffee plantations and began organic farming of coffee. Integrated pest management was widely adopted in the grain producing areas. Other national institutions began to get involved: the Nicaragua Autonomous University (UNAM) gave technical support to integrated pest management; The Nicaraguan Womens' association (AMNLAE) began programmes with peasant women, and the National Union of Farmers and Ranchers (UNAG) began helping cooperative development.

The programme has now extended to cover 35 cooperatives. Seven people, all Nicaraguans, are employed on the project and new components are being added. These include the protection of the last remnants of the natural Caribbean pine forests that extend into the area, the farming of green iguanas to replenish wild populations, the introduction of a greater variety of tree crops and alley cropping for corn and bean production.

The ecosystems of the area have not been restored, but the degradation has been halted. There is a tendency towards more sustainable farming practices and a slight increase in tree cover. The significant thing is that this has been accomplished by the peasants themselves with only minor outside economic incentives. All decision making has been local and the people have contributed their work and enthusiasm to changing agricultural practices and carrying out land conservation programmes.

Source: IUCN project staff in Nicaragua and Costa Rica.

CASE STUDY 8

Rural development programme for the Korup National Park Area

Korup National Park, in Cameroon, covers 125,900ha in an area of forest that has never been logged. A total of 252 bird species have been observed in the park and its immediate vicinity, which is also exceptionally important for primate conservation and very rich botanically. Korup was declared Cameroon's first rainforest national park on 30 October 1986.

There is a moderately dense human population living in the immediate vicinity of the new national park, and 1,042 people live in six villages within its boundaries. According to the legal decree under which the park was established, these villagers will have to be resettled.

It is accepted that the long-term future of the park can only be assured if efforts are made to carry out this resettlement with minimum inconvenience to the people. The project will need to take into account social and economic problems which could result from resettlement.

Resettlement will be based on knowledge of the socio-economic situation of the villages of Korup and the surrounding area, resulting from surveys now being carried out. At present the main land use activities of the people living within the park differ according to the traditions of the two major ethnic groups, their tribal affinities outside the park and local soil conditions.

The east of the national park is inhabited by Bantu tribes: the Bima, the Bakoko and the Ngolo. They live on richer, older volcanic soils. Cocoa and coffee are grown together with perennial tree crops such as mango and avocado pear. This cultivation has made relatively little impact on the park as a whole.

In the western portion of the park the population is made up of two non-Bantu tribes: the Korup and the Ejagham. The Korup constitute 61.5% of the population of the park as a whole. The soils of the area they inhabit are extremely infertile; consequently, the Korup people have traditionally subsisted by hunting and fishing. Today they tend to be professional hunters and the main Korup village of Erat is the centre of the bush-meat trade. The majority of the Korup tribe lives in Nigeria and cross-border trade and wildlife smuggling are features of the local life. Forest products traded with Nigeria include dried endocarps of seeds of *Ricinodendron heudelotii*, *Panda oleosa*, and *Irvingia gabonensis*. Fermented sap from raffia palm *Rapphia monbuttorum*, is distilled to make illicit gin.

The rural development programme for the Korup region incorporates the protection and management of the park and its development as a tourist attraction. Meeting the needs of the people living in, and close to the park is seen as a priority. Potential areas for resettlement have been identified in two regions adjacent to the park through which new roads are planned. Nurseries, to provide seedlings of indigenous food crops, cash crops, fruit trees and fuelwood, will be set up in these resettlement areas and near the park headquarters in Mundemba. Villages will be resettled as the necessary socio-economic studies are completed and new infrastructures such as roads, village sites, nurseries and farms are developed.

The Korup project involves cooperation between an unusual number of different government departments, as well as NGOs and bilateral aid agencies. National parks in Cameroon are under the official jurisdiction of the Secretariat of State for Tourism but, because of the development nature of the project, other ministries have also been involved. Significantly, the Ministry of Planning sees the project as a model for similar rural development and conservation schemes elsewhere in the country.

The project has benefited from much more external financial support than other projects of its kind. A considerable amount of information has been acquired on the natural history, natural resources and social conditions in the park and its surroundings. Some development work at the village level has been accomplished in the buffer zone, mainly the introduction of agroforestry techniques on a pilot scale. But none of the people living within the park have yet been persuaded to move to the buffer zone and it is not clear if the rural development work has had any real impact on the conservation problems of the park.

Resources applied to the improvement of the infrastructure and protection of the park itself have produced a notable improvement in the conservation status of the area. But this is a good example of a project where it has proved extremely difficult to move buffer zone activities from the conceptual and data gathering stages to the point where they contribute to real conservation achievement on the ground.

Source: Republic of Cameroon (undated) The Korup Project: Plan for developing the Korup National Park and its support zone. WWF, Godalming, UK.

Tree Crops and Agroforestry in Buffer Zones

Agricultural systems that include a large number and variety of trees provide the soil and watershed functions required in buffer zones and come closer than other intensive production systems to providing habitats for a diversity of fauna and flora. This is especially so when indigenous tree species are used. The nutrient cycling efficiency of deep rooted trees and the ability of may leguminous trees to fix nitrogen are essential elements in efforts to stabilise shifting agriculture. In many high rainfall tropical areas with steep slopes and nutrient poor soils, tree crops and tree dominated agroforestry systems are the only stable form of land use other than natural forest.

Most traditional farmers in moist forest areas are very well aware of the value of trees. Shifting cultivators retain many tree species which either provide products or enhance soil fertility. Sedentary farmers grow a variety of trees in "home gardens" around their dwellings; these produce fruits, wood, fibres, spices, medicines, etc. Agroforestry as a scientific discipline is relatively new, but as a way of life in the tropics, it has existed for millenia.

Agroforestry has so many features which make it attractive for the stabilising of land use in buffer zones that it has sometimes been regarded as a magic formula for success. In reality, bringing about changes in the ways in which rural people use trees in their farming systems presents the same problems as any other form of rural development activity. The innovations have to correspond to the aspirations of the people and they have to yield more for the work invested in their establishment than any alternative activity.

Many tree crops and multi-purpose trees provide products for local use. Others yield crops which can be marketed further afield. At times world prices for the commodities produced by tropical tree crops are high and they appear to offer possibilities for generating significant income. The temptation to promote the planting of these crops in buffer zones is then very great. In the event that commodity prices remain high, such crops would indeed be an attractive option for buffer zones. They would create stable employment on a fixed area of land whilst constituting a physical feature or barrier around the protected area and providing valuable watershed protection functions.

Unfortunately tropical tree crop commodity prices have been subject to marked fluctuations and are highly susceptible to variations in supply and demand from other regions. Marginally better climatic conditions and better management have enabled Southeast Asian countries to produce palm oil much more cheaply than their African competitors. Major past investments in palm oil in Africa are now losing money and some are being abandoned. The price of robusta coffee from the lowland tropics of Africa is at an all-time low since the market has the option of buying the preferred arabica coffee from the uplands of Central and South America. Clove producers in Africa are at the mercy of Indonesian producers who control 90 per cent of the world trade. Huge new investments in cacao plantations in Southeast Asia pose a serious threat to producers in West Africa.

The consequences for protected area buffer zones of sudden collapses in commodity prices are demonstrated by the failure of the oil palm industry adjacent to the Korup National Park in Cameroon and the tea industry in the Usambara Mountains. Depressed palm oil prices led to the laying-off of many workers from oil palm estates located on the boundary of Korup. The people had come to the area a generation ago to work on the estates and had nowhere else to go and no alternative source of employment. Many took up small scale farming, much of it damaging to the forests. In the Usambaras, many tea estate workers could not survive on the government controlled salaries and took up cardamom cultivation in the forests. Many tea estate workers around the Sinharaja Reserve in Sri Lanka also began farming in the forests when earnings from tea declined.

Monocultures of tree crops are also susceptible to disease. The *Monilia* pod-rot of cacao has caused the collapse of cacao farming in the Talamanca District of Costa Rica. Many farmers who previously made a good living from cacao have now been forced to revert to shifting cultivation in the forested hills.

Guidelines

21   **Agroforestry and tree crops can be highly appropriate uses of land in buffer zones. Systems using indigenous trees and those that use a large number and variety of trees are particularly good at providing buffer zone functions.**

22   **Agroforestry and tree crop innovations can be introduced and promoted through standard rural development mechanisms but the same constraints apply to them as to any other form of rural development activity.**

23   **Systems which produce a variety of products for local use will be more stable than those producing a single crop for distant markets. Excessive dependence on a single cash crop should be viewed with caution.**

24   **Existing knowledge and use of trees should be fully exploited. Many traditional societies make extensive use of trees in shifting cultivation systems and the full extent of this use may only become apparent to outside advisers after a considerable time.**

25   **Buffer zones provide an opportunity to preserve traditional land-races of tree crops, fruit trees and multipurpose trees. Wherever possible buffer zone projects should promote the use of these local varieties and avoid introducing exotic species, or even exotic varieties of local species.**

Further Reading

Cook, C.C. and Grut, M. 1989. Agroforestry in Sub-Saharan Africa, a Farmers Perspective.

FAO. 1985. *Monitoring and Evaluation of Participatory Forestry Projects*. FAO Forestry Paper No. 60, FAO, Rome, Italy.

FAO/East West Centre. Undated. Community forestry: Lessons from case ctudies the Asia Pacific Region. FAO, Bangkok, Thailand.

Huxley, P.A. (Ed.) 1983. *Plant Research and Agroforestry.* ICRAF, Nairobi.

Pant, M.M. 1986. *Forestry for Economic Development*. Medhawi Publishers, Dehradun. World Bank, Washington, DC.

FAO. 1985. *Tree Growing by Rural People*. FAO Forestry Paper 64. FAO, Rome.

Wiensum, K.F. (Ed.) 1989. *Strategies and Designs for Afforestation, Reforestation and Tree Planting*. Pudec Wageningen, The Netherlands.

CASE STUDY 9

The Arfak Mountains Nature Reserve, Irian Jaya

The Arfak Mountains Nature Reserve covers 45,000ha of primary tropical rainforest in the Bird's Head region of Irian Jaya. It is planned to extend the reserve to 70,000ha at which stage it will include 80% of the traditional territory of the indigenous Hatam people.

In order to build local support for the reserve, a system of nature reserve management areas (NRMA) has been introduced. These consist of the land owned by loose local groupings of the Hatam, each speaking the same dialect and having traditions of cooperation. Thirteen NRMAs have been formed, each headed by a committee of local people. Outside assistance is channelled through the NRMAs to projects outside the reserve boundary in what is known as a "Community Development Zone". Small-scale technical, financial and material support is provided to the NRMAs for activities which include agroforestry, butterfly farming, fishing ponds, fruit and vegetable growing, introduction of garden terracing and cover crops. (Cover crops are leguminous herbs or low shrubs which protect the soil surface, stifle weeds and enrich the soil in nitrates during fallow periods between other crops.)

The NRMA committees took part in the identification and marking of the reserve boundary and assistance to them is conditional on their respect for this boundary. They are allowed to collect forest produce within the reserves but house-building and gardening is restricted to the community development zone outside the reserve.

Further Reading
Craven, I. 1990. Arfak Mountains Management Plan. WWF Jakarta.
Petolz, R.G. 1991. Conservation and development in Irian Jaya. E.J. Buill, Leiden, The Netherlands

CASE STUDY 10

Agroforestry and conservation at Bawang Ling, Hainan, China

In Hainan, China, shifting cultivation, rubber plantations and timber exploitation for export to the mainland have reduced tropical moist forest to a few remnants in the upper lowland and montane zones. Bawang Ling Nature Reserve, situated in the west of the region, is one of the best remaining areas of intact natural forest. It is of outstanding conservation importance.

Around Bawang Ling is a transitional zone of different vegetation types which buffers the intact forest core. The transitional zone links the strictly protected core zone or conservation area to cultivated land through a series of vegetation and crop types of increasing simplicity and intensity of human impact. The buffer zone consists of selectively logged oak-dipterocarp forest and forest enriched with *Litchis chinensis*. Some degraded scrub and grassland is partly planted with *Cunninghamia* and *Pinus*. A little further away (about 2km from the core forest) are agroforestry plantations and the agricultural land of Bawang Ling village.

The agroforestry plantations are experimental schemes being developed by local forestry and agricultural stations. They consist mainly of teak under-planted with cardamom, camphor *Cinnamomum camphora* and other species including *Lannea grandis* used as a substrate for growing mushrooms. The experimental programme is being further developed to produce mixed crops of trees, shrubs and perennial and annual field crops.

The core and buffer areas of Bawang Ling are being used as an integrated ecosystem research programme under a MAB scheme carried out by Academia Sinica and German research institutes. The long-term objectives of the research programme are to determine:

● the critical factors which control ecosystem function, stability and productivity in terms of human needs;

● how durable the ecosystems of different design are and how they can be sustained;

● the impacts of any kind and intensity of reduction of species richness, diversity and complexity;

● optimal models for sustained management of ecosystems at the level of natural or man-made forests, village, region or economic sector.

Source: Eberhard F. Bruenig and Huang Ya-Kwen at the World Forest Institute, Hamburg and in Hainan.

CASE STUDY 11

Boundary strips around Dumoga Bone National Park, Sulawezi

Dumoga Bone, with an area of some 30,000ha, is surrounded by an adjoining natural forest of over 200,000ha. These forests are subject to selective logging and some are scheduled to be converted to agriculture. The main strategy for the park is to extend its boundaries, to keep as much natural forest around the park as possible and to develop the forest outside the park as a buffer zone. Where agricultural land extends to the park border, the buffer zone programme includes boundary strip planting for a total of some 200km around the park's perimeter. These plantings consist of a small strip of 5m or less width on the park boundary and their aim is to clearly define the boundary. Local farmers are also approached and asked to give permission for extending the boundary strip on their land for at least some 20-30m. Government subsidies are available for planting species of the farmers' choice and the progamme is backed up through recommendations made by the park administration. The programme is therefore implemented with the cooperation of the local government and the farmers owning adjacent land. Farmers participating in the scheme are also given the right to extract firewood and collect fruits in the buffer strip, but they are expected to maintain the 1-5m strip inside the park, working with the park personnel.

The width of at least 20m allows for satellite monitoring of the forest. Such monitoring should, for example, reveal whether buffer zone management will lead to enhanced integrity of the park. A base study is also planned to rate park integrity by species richness, occurrence of key species, forest structure, degree of human influence and other key factors.

Use of exotic species has been restricted to the area outside the park. *Gliricidia* has been successfully propagated from stumps to set sharp boundary lines, at the border of the park where the endangered maleo bird *Macrocephalon maleo* buries its eggs for hatching in hot soils. *Calliandra,* a widely used firewood species, is planted as seedlings and can compete with alang alang grass *Imperata sp.* but will also invade secondary vegetation and open areas within the park and elsewhere.

Source: Jan Wind in Bogor, Indonesia

CASE STUDY 12

Managing a buffer zone around the Cyclops Mountains Nature Reserve, Irian Jaya, Indonesia

The Cyclops Mountains Nature Reserve is an area of officially protected forest, ranging from sea level to approximately 1,880m on the north coast of Irian Jaya. The mountainous reserve covers about 30,000ha adjacent to Jayapura (the provincial capital) and includes numerous small farming communities and housing settlements. Indigenous ownership of the reserve lands by the Imbi, Tabla and Sentani tribal groups is disputed by the government and this conflict has frustrated previous attempts at reserve management. Recently, efforts have been made to reconcile traditional land ownership, conservation, and community development needs.

The reserve is the water catchment area of the capital and surrounding region. Water conservation (with its socio-cultural and development implications) has been identified by tribal councils and landowners as well as local government as the strongest justification for the nature reserve. Extension and conservation efforts are concentrated on strengthening this 'common ground' by protecting the vital water catchment function of the reserve. Economic incentives are employed to stabilise the boundary of the reserve, through certain buffer zone activities. These may be linked directly to water resources (for example, a network of over 100 fish ponds), or indirectly, by concentrating agricultural production and diversifying agroforestry systems. Communities around the reserve have already marked more than half of the boundary themselves using strips of *Cordyline* plants, nutmeg and other fruit trees, and furniture-grade timber species. This living boundary can itself be managed for sustainable yields. The location of the boundary was chosen by tribal council leaders representing traditional landowners. Although it is based on current and projected indigenous land needs, the boundary largely coincides with the original government-designated line.

In certain areas, buffer zone development is used as a management tool to solve encroachment problems. The zone provides an income-bearing alternative to destructive shifting agriculture within the reserve. This approach of identifying a conservation rationale based on local priorities, establishing a boundary chosen by the community, and using buffer zone development to reduce or eliminate demands on the reserve, serves as a culturally appropriate, equitable and humane example of conservation management.

Source: Stephen V. Nash, WWF Indonesia

CASE STUDY 13

Improved farming techniques around the Monteverde Cloud Forest Reserve in Costa Rica

Soil erosion and wildlife habitat destruction have resulted from excessive clearing of forest on the Pacific slopes below the Monteverde Reserve in Costa Rica. The Monteverde Conservation League has embarked upon a programme to encourage greater use of indigenous trees in agricultural land. The programme covers an area of about six kilometres by ten kilometres and has a population of 3,000 people. 20 local farmers participated in the scheme in 1989 and 40 in 1990; the farmers elected a committee to discuss ways of improving agricultural practices. This committee worked with two foresters and ten junior extension workers employed by the league. Two nurseries were established and these produce 125,000 trees per year. In the past most of the trees planted in the area were exotic cypresses and casuarinas; the intention is to reduce these to 20% of the nursery production and to concentrate on indigenous species.

Windbreaks are important in local agriculture: they boost milk yields by up to 50%.

In the past exotic species were used, but recent research has shown that two local species, *Citharexylum integerrimum* and *Acnistus arborescens*, are equally effective; and in addition their fruits provide food for at least 23 species of indigenous birds.

Windbreaks also improve the productivity of the land for other crops. The league is examining the possibility of improving coffee growing in these areas using organic farming techniques. They are negotiating with distributors in the USA to gain access to high price markets for coffee produced without the use of pesticides. The distributors will return US$1 to the league for every pound of coffee sold.

Source: Jim Crisp, Monteverde Conservation League, Costa Rica.

CASE STUDY 14

Fruit tree development in the Talamanca Region in Costa Rica

The Talamanca District covers 2,800km² in the southeastern part of Costa Rica. It extends from the Caribbean coast to 3,800m high volcanic peaks on the continental divide. Much of the area is forested, and includes two national parks, one biological reserve and five indigenous peoples' reserves. The forests are highly diverse and are the habitat of several rare and endangered species. About 25,000 people live in the district; roughly 56% work in industrial banana production and various sorts of farming on alluvial soils along the Sixaola river on the Panamanian border; 26% work in tourism, fishing and agriculture along the coast. Until recently cacao farming was the main source of income for this sector of the community. The remaining 16% of the population are indigenous peoples living from maize, rice and bean cultivation, and harvesting forest products in the hills.

A *Monilia* fungal disease of ripening cacao pods, combined with low prices has seriously depressed the economy of the area in recent years. This has forced people into much greater dependence on forest products, and particularly on shifting cultivation in forested areas.

A local NGO, ANAI has been working in Talamanca for about ten years with the objective of "Integrating conservation of the natural ecosystem with the development needs of rural peoples". ANAI had its origins at a time when this part of Costa Rica was a centre of the "hippy" culture of the 1960s. The acronym derives from the Association of New Alchemists Inc. but the word "anai" means "friends" in the local Bribri language and the link with hippies and alchemists is purely historical. ANAI has been active throughout the province and has tackled various agricultural, forestry, fisheries and social issues. One of the more interesting programmes was to encourage greater use of a wider variety of tree species. Small communities were provided with technical guidance, materials, seedlings and help in organising community tree nurseries. Over 100 tree species, some local but many from other parts of the tropics, were made available through ANAI: about 75 of these were fruit trees. ANAI did not attempt to impose any particular species on the people; they were encouraged to experiment with many species and make their own choices. Initially, in spite of the disease problems and weak market, the nurseries concentrated on producing cacao seedlings. This was partly because the people were traditional cacao growers, and partly because they hoped that new varieties available through ANAI, would be resistant to *Monilia*.

Recently, cacao has gone out of favour and there is more interest in alternative tree crops. Many farmers now grow a greater variety of trees on their land than they did before ANAI became active. In most cases, however, this is limited to a few individual trees of several fruit species growing near houses for personal consumption, and they have not had a significant economic impact.

A few species are also now being grown for cash. The Brazilian fruit "araza" (Myrtaceae) is widely sold to local hotels and restaurants for juice making. In addition, "guanabana" *Annona muricata* (Annonaceae), "carambola" *Averrhoa carambola* (Oxalidaceae) and "rambutans" *Nephelium lappaceum* (Sapindaceae) are being grown on a commercial scale. However, ANAI consider that the most important achievement to date has been the greater thoughtfulness and increased willingness to experiment and accept change. This has emerged amongst the population as a result of their involvement in the planning and management of the tree nurseries and in the various other promotional activities of ANAI.

Source: Rafael Ocampo, IUCN/ANAI Talamanca, Alejandro Imbach, Turrialba, Costa Rica and Wells *et al* 1990.

5 BUFFER ZONES IN FORESTED LANDS

In those areas of the tropics where extensive areas of natural forest still persist, the problems of buffer zone management are quite different from those in densely settled areas. National parks and reserves in Amazonia, the Zaïre-Congo Basin and parts of Indonesia and Papua New Guinea are often surrounded by natural forests which for practical purposes are indistinguishable from the forests in the protected areas. The term buffer zone is seldom employed for such areas, but these forests fulfill the functions of buffer zones better than any other land use.

The only measure that is required to consolidate this buffer zone function is to anticipate and pre-empt any changes in land use which may occur in the future. It is particularly important to take measures to prevent spontaneous, unplanned occupation of the area by agricultural colonists. To achieve this the land must be allocated to a specified use. Various categories of use allocation are commonly employed and give different degrees of protection. The categories of partial reserve given on pages 7 and 8 often provide the best protection and leave open the option for ecologically sound development at some future date. They also place the land under the authority of the protected area management agency, which is thus able to control all activities in the buffer zone.

Government authorities may feel that designation of such reserve status would be too restrictive of future resource use. In this situation it is important that the decision on allocation takes into account the need to maintain the buffering function. Various categories of land will provide these functions particularly well. Land which is permanently allocated for sustained yield selective logging, or harvesting of non-wood products, will, if well managed, provide an excellent near-natural habitat to buffer a totally protected area. Lands which are allocated for the exclusive use of indigenous peoples, and where non-traditional uses and changes in land use are effectively restricted, will also provide excellent buffer zones. However, with improved communications, the aspirations of even the most isolated traditional communities can be expected to evolve. Total transfer of authority over land to such communities, on the grounds that their present lifestyle is ecologically sustainable, may result in conservation problems in the future. Any unsustainable activities of these people must be subject to the same restrictions that apply to any other sector of society.

State-owned land adjacent to a protected area should not be sold or otherwise alienated to individuals or corporations from outside the immediate area. Neither should it be allocated for colonisation or resettlement schemes or for industrial development. The only exception to this principle could be where reputable private foundations or nature conservation organisations acquire the land in order to manage it for nature conservation. However, even this form of conservation management can be equally well achieved through the negotiation of management agreements on government owned land. There may be circumstances where there is some compelling reason for forest land adjacent to protected areas to pass into private hands. In this situation government should restrict changes in the use of the land and should require that a prescribed proportion remains under natural forest cover.

Guidelines

26 **Governments should retain and consolidate control over state forest lands adjacent to protected areas. This can best be achieved by legally gazetting them as various categories of partial reserves, forest reserves or indigenous peoples' reserves.**

27 **Forests permanently allocated for sustained yield selective timber extraction can make excellent buffer zones, providing management standards are high.**

28 **Any alienation of forest land to the private sector must carry a requirement that a prescribed percentage remains under natural forest cover. Any subsequent changes in land use must be approved by appropriate local planning authorities, who must consult the protected area management agency.**

29 **Forests allocated for the use of indigenous peoples should benefit from some controls on their use. Restrictions should apply to any unsustainable harvesting or hunting techniques and to changes in land use.**

Further Reading

Johns, A.D. 1985. Selective logging and wildlife conservation in tropical rain forest: Problems and recommendations. *Conservation Biology* **31**: 355-75.

Poore, D. and Sayer, J. 1987. *The Management of Tropical Moist Forest Lands: Ecological Guidelines.* IUCN, Gland, Switzerland and Cambridge, UK.

Buffer Zones and Forest-dwelling Peoples

Some of the more extensive tropical forest areas of the world are inhabited by small populations of people whose way of life has been little influenced by the outside world. These people, minorities in their own countries, typically have little influence with the government institutions who take decisions about the use of forest lands. There have been many instances where national parks or nature reserves have been established without consideration of the consequences for indigenous populations. Traditional hunting and gathering practices that have continued for generations suddenly become criminal offences as a consequence of laws passed in a distant city. Such situations are rarer nowadays and many governments have established programmes to safeguard the rights of people who wish to retain a traditional way of life. But there are still many places in the tropical forest zone where protected area managers need to work with indigenous populations, both within the protected areas and especially in surrounding buffer zones.

Indigenous forest peoples have an enormous accumulated knowledge of forest ecosystems and the products that can be obtained from them. They have often developed techniques for living off the forest in ways which conserve stocks of the resources that they are exploiting. This knowledge is of increasing value to society at large - it can be put to use by the pharmaceutical industry, forest ecologists and, not least, by the managers of protected areas and buffer zones. But when population densities exceed a certain level the sustainability of the practices of indigenous peoples often breaks down. This is especially the case when colonisation or exploitation of their land by outside farmers or loggers forces them to concentrate in smaller or less suitable forest areas than those to which they are adapted. And indigenous peoples will not remain immune to modern influences on their lifestyles: many will wish to share the social and technological advances that they observe in other sectors of society.

As populations have exceeded the carrying capacity of the land, hill tribe peoples in India, Burma, Thailand and Indo-China, practising traditional forms of shifting agriculture, have destroyed vast areas of forest and left behind huge expanses of degraded land. Indigenous people armed with modern weapons have greatly reduced wildlife populations in large areas of Africa. There are relatively few situations where indigenous peoples will be able to continue to pursue their traditional lifestyles in the forest in a stable and sustainable way in the medium term future. In most cases it is inevitable that they will evolve into a closer association with mainstream society. They should be helped to do this in a way which allows them to enjoy the benefits of modern society whilst retaining those aspects of their culture and lifestyles which are of value to them.

The needs and wishes of indigenous communities must be taken into account at the very earliest stages of establishment of protected areas. National parks and other categories of totally protected area will often not be the most effective means of achieving conservation objectives in areas inhabited by indigenous peoples. Attempts to move populations to new areas have usually caused misery and social unrest; the protected areas have been resented and their resources abused.

The optimum strategy will often be to make extensive use of the various categories of partially protected areas where people may continue their traditional practices, reserving total protection only for those sites which are of critical importance for biological diversity. The worst option is to establish large totally protected areas with dense populations of deprived displaced persons struggling to survive on their periphery. Many of the problems of buffer zone management can be avoided by adequate consultation and careful planning at the stage when the boundaries of the protected area are first delimited.

This planning period may need to be long. It is important to have as much information as possible on the way local people use the forest and its resources. The social and political structures of the people must be respected and their cultural needs considered alongside their material requirements. Planning must be based upon a dialogue with the people that ensures that the perspectives of all sectors of their society are represented.

In conducting this dialogue it is particularly important that traditional systems of representation and decision making be respected. Local institutions and processes should as far as possible be incorporated into permanent structures that will guarantee peoples' participation in the management of the protected area and its buffer zone.

The value of preserving the rights of specific named communities has been recognised by the National Parks and Wildlife Office of the Sarawak Forest Department. The local Iban will benefit from legally-recognised rights to exclusive access to the natural resources of substantial areas of forest around the Lanjak-Entimau Wildlife Sanctuary. The Iban will thus have an interest in preventing outside groups from over-exploiting these resources.

Guidelines

30 **Indigenous peoples' rights and aspirations must be considered early and throughout the process of establishing new protected areas and buffer zones. Options for achieving conservation objectives through a balance of small total reserves located in larger areas of partial reserves must be thoroughly explored.**

31 **Indigenous peoples must participate in the the planning and management of the protected area and its buffer zone. The process of dialogue with the communities should be conducted through traditional decision making processes and institutions.**

32 **Traditional rights to use resources in buffer zones should be maintained and may be improved upon; access to these resources by non-local people should be restricted. However, provision must be made to restrict resource use by indigenous peoples if this attains a level where the sustainability of the resource is threatened.**

33 **The protected area authority should be associated with measures to improve the quality of life of the indigenous communities in ways which are consistent with the attainment of conservation objectives. Revenues generated by tourism in the protected area should be applied to such programmes. Indigenous communities should be favoured for employment opportunities in the protected area and should be encouraged to offer products and services to visitors.**

Further Reading

Denslow, J.S. and Padoch, C. 1988. *People of the Tropical Rain Forest.* University of California Press, Berkeley, Los Angeles, London and Smithsonian Institution, Washington, DC.
McNeely, J.A. and Pitt, D. 1985. *Culture and Conservation: The Human Dimension in Environmental Planning.* Croom Helm, London.

CASE STUDY 15

Manu National Park, Peru

Manu National Park on the Amazonian slopes of the Peruvian Andes is one of the most biologically diverse protected areas in the world. It covers 1,532,806ha of mountains and lowland rainforest most of which is unaltered by modern man. At least four different groups of indigenous people live in the park. These include the Machinguenga, Yaminahua, Amahuaca and Mashco-Piros. These forest Indians are nomadic and until recently have lived in harmony with nature in the area. They grow rootcrops along rivers and lake shores, and hunt and gather all their other needs from the forests. Taboos restrict the hunting of certain species and thus help to avoid over-exploitation.

Park regulations allow these groups to remain within the park and practice their traditional activities. This appears to be largely compatible with conserving the biodiversity of the park, although problems have occurred with one group of Machinguengas who have settled at the site of an old mission station and hunt commercially using weapons given to them by the missionaries.

The strategy adopted by the park authorities has been to attempt to define exclusive hunting territories for such Indian groups and to encourage others to relocate to indigenous reserves to the north west and south east of the park. The park authorities protect both the buffer zone, indigenous reserves and the park itself against encroachment or exploitation by people who are not native to the area.

Source: Luis Angel and Alejandro Imbach, Lima Peru and Turrialba, Costa Rica.

CASE STUDY 16

Kuna Indians and jungle tourism in Panama

In the early 1980s, the Kuna Indians of Panama set aside an area of primary forest along the southern border of their territory - the Comarca of Kuna Yala - as a wildlife reserve. The core of this "Kuna Park" covers 60,000ha and is situated about three hours drive from Panama City.

The Kuna have attempted to develop cultural and natural history tourism in this park. The initiative was seen as a potential model for ways in which similar indigenous groups in other parts of the tropics might improve their living standards whilst conserving the forests in which they live.

Since the area is only a short distance from Panama City, it could theoretically receive large numbers of foreign visitors. The islands off the coast are accessible by air and a steady flow of tourists visit them, mainly for their coastal and cultural attractions. Attempts to develop nature tourism around the Nusagandi Field Station in the mainland forests have been less successful.

One fundamental problem was that the 25km of road linking the Inter-American Highway from the Nusagandi Camp was never improved for access by ordinary rental vehicles. The road beyond Nusagandi leading 21km to the coast was in worse condition being almost impassible at times. The facilities at Nusagandi are quite basic and may not have met the levels of comfort expected by even hardy "ecotourists". In recent years the political situation in Panama has made it a relatively less attractive destination for North American tourists than its peaceful neighbour, Costa Rica. The Panamanian Tourist Institute has focussed on the more sophisticated pleasures of Panama City and the beach resorts and has done little to promote nature tourism. The result is that what was heralded as a flagship project has been a relative failure and tourists have preferred to go to intrinsically less interesting areas with better access and infrastructures.

Source: Houseal, B.C. *et al.* 1985. Indigenous cultures and protected areas in Central America. *Cultural Survival Quarterly* **9**(1):15-18.
Breslin, P and Chapin, M. 1986. Conservation Kuna style in Annis, S and P. Hakim, *Grassroots Development in Latin America* **9**(2): 26-35. Lynne Rienner Publishers, Boulder and London.

CASE STUDY 17

Local opposition to the Loagan Bunut National Park, Sarawak

The Berawan people of Long Teru, Sarawak are opposed to the creation of the Loagan Bunut National Park on their traditional lands. They have announced in a public appeal that, "Our land is our survival and to take it away from us would mean the extermination of our people".

Loagan Bunut is Sarawak's only natural lake. It is rich in fish and other wildlife. The proposed National Park would cover 10,740ha of land and the boundaries may include undisturbed peat-swamp forest. The lake itself cannot be expected to survive in its present form if the surrounding catchment areas are radically altered. Currently, road-building and logging are threatening natural habitats in the area where competition for land is intense.

The traditional economy of the Berawan is based on hunting, gathering, fishing and shifting cultivation. The people are clearly aware of the loss of the natural resources on which they depend, but also resent any interference with their customary rights to utilise the land. The announcement of the new National Park in an official proclamation noted that the erection of buildings, hunting, the cutting of vegetation and the clearing of land were all to be prohibited within the National Park. Unfortunately the Berawan had not been consulted about the restrictions and, as a consequence are not prepared to cooperate in conservation plans for the area.

Sources: Kavanagh, M. 1985. Planning considerations for a system of national parks and wildlife sanctuaries in Sarawak. *Sarawak Gazette* **111**(1491): 15-29.
Marcus Colchester, Survival International, London.

Forest Management in Buffer Zones

Any logging of natural forests carries with it the risk of disruption of ecological functions and the loss of species. The vast majority of species in tropical forests are invertebrates: the insect faunas of forest canopies are especially rich. Almost nothing is known of the effect of even light selective logging on this fauna. The biological interactions between species are so complex in tropical forests that the loss of even a few seemingly unimportant species may have repercussions on the life cycles of other more conspicuous, or economically valuable species.

Notwithstanding this, studies of the vertebrate fauna of logged forests have shown that forest ecosystems are more resilient than one might have supposed. And whatever views one might hold on industrial forestry, it is certainly true that even a logged-over forest must constitute a much better buffer zone than an area from which the forest has been totally cleared. In principle, and according to the forestry legislation in virtually every tropical country, forests managed for timber should be less susceptible to invasion by shifting farmers than forests which are not allocated for timber production. In countries such as Burma, which has so far had a long history of good forest management, the production forests are still forested but most of the un-logged forests of the uplands and distant parts of the country have been totally cleared for agriculture. However, in other parts of the tropics, especially in insular Southeast Asia, West Africa and parts of South America, logging has very frequently been followed by the clearance of the land for unsustainable agriculture.

The impact of industrial forestry on buffer zone functions varies enormously according to the type of forest and the social and economic conditions of the country. Where forests contain few commercially valuable species, as in the Zaïre-Congo forest block where only one or two trees per hectare are extracted, the impact of logging on biological diversity is slight. These lightly logged forests contain higher populations of elephants, various antelopes and some primates than unlogged forests. In the dipterocarp forests of Southeast Asia where over one hundred cubic metres of timber are often removed per hectare, the impacts are obviously much greater. In West Africa where forest departments are weak and population pressure high, logged forests are almost invariably encroached upon by farmers. In Central Africa the population is sparse, demand for land low, and agricultural encroachment is only a localised problem. In parts of Southeast Asia forest departments are strong enough to keep small farmers out of the forest, even where demand for land is high. But throughout the tropics one of the most important environmental problems of our day is the difficulty of preventing shifting cultivators from ravaging forests after logging. Every buffer zone situation must therefore be assessed separately.

The implications of different strategies for managing timber production forests in buffer zones have been examined in detail by Harris (1984). Harris's work was mainly carried out in the Western Cascade Mountains in the USA, but many of his findings apply equally to situations in the tropics, especially where traditional land use is practised. His work has important implications for buffer zones:

"... an extensive approach founded on principles of landscape and regional ecology, must be developed to complement the 'intensive' approach represented by national parks and wildlife refuges. This argument is based upon the premise that multiple-use management requires that several products be given consideration, but it does not require that the products be considered equally. This concept allows for an inverse relation between the relative importance of several products in the management zone being considered. As one product (e.g. biological diversity) becomes relatively less important as we move outward from the core area, a second product (e.g. wood) becomes relatively more important. Thus the importance ranking of the various objectives is dependent on distance removed from the core area.

A second corollary is that the size and degree of protection accorded the core area should also be directly proportional to the intensity with which the human dominated landscape is managed and inversely proportional to the amount of surrounding buffer area. If low intensity forest management (e.g. long rotation selection felling) were to dominate the landscape matrix, then requirements for totally natural areas would be much less than if the landscape consisted of tree plantations or agricultural crops. If it were possible to manage the entire forest landscape in a very low-intensity, long-rotation manner, there would be little if any need for special protection areas".

IUCN and the International Tropical Timber Organization have recently completed a review of biological diversity conservation measures applicable to forests managed for timber production (IUCN/ITTO, in press). This study will lead to the production of *Guidelines for Biodiversity Conservation in Managed Tropical Forests*, which will be adopted by the ITTO in 1991. These guidelines will suggest measures that should be applied to all timber-producing forests that are adjacent to protected areas. The study concludes that the control of logging personnel, prevention of post-logging encroachment, retention of small undisturbed forest refuges and protection of keystone tree species, such as palms and figs, are fundamental to maintaining the biodiversity value of logged forests.

Guidelines

34 The choice of forest management system to be used in a buffer zone must take into account the requirements of biological diversity conservation. In general, selective systems will be more compatible with conservation objectives than clear-felling or uniform systems.

35 The status of forest cover and of wildlife populations should be monitored in the logged forest. This monitoring should focus on indicator species when these are known; insectivorous birds may be among the most useful indicators.

36 Fig trees, various palms and large "over-mature" trees which are not commercial timber species often play critical roles in maintaining biological cycles. These and other "keystone" species should be specially protected during logging operations and should not be eliminated by post-logging silvicultural practices.

37 Logging regulations to ensure the sustainability of management must be rigorously enforced in buffer zones. Logging personnel must be provided with meat rations and prevented from hunting; check points must be established on logging tracks to prevent access by poachers or shifting farmers and roads and bridges must be closed-off after logging ceases.

38 Islands of undisturbed forest must be left covering at least five per cent of the forest area and these must be located so as to cover representative areas of all forest types.

39 The protected area management agency, if it is not the forest department, must be involved in the negotiation of logging concession terms and must have legal authority to intervene to defend conservation interests in managed forests which are adjacent to protected areas.

Further Reading

FAO. 1989. *Review of Forest Management Systems in Tropical Asia.* FAO Forestry Paper, 89. FAO Rome, Italy.

FAO. 1989b. *Management of Tropical Moist Forests in Africa.* FAO Forestry Paper, 88. FAO, Rome, Italy.

Ffolliot, P.F. and Thomas, J.L. 1983. *Environmentally Sound Small-scale Forestry Projects. Guidelines for planning.* CODEL/VITA publications. Arlington, VA.

Harris, L.D. 1984. *The Fragmented Forest. Island Biogeography Theory and the Preservation of Biotic Diversity.* Chicago University Press, Chicago and London.

Lamprecht, H. 1989. *Silviculture in the Tropics.* GTZ, Eschborn, Germany.

Poore, D. 1989. *No Forest Without Trees.* Earthscan, London.

IUCN/ITTO. (In prep.) Conserving biodiversity in managed tropical forests. IUCN, Gland, Switzerland and Cambridge, UK.

BOX 4

Natural Forest Management Systems

Natural forest management systems are based on techniques to promote natural regeneration of desirable timber species. Five conditions have been identified for successful forest management programmes; these are especially important for timber extraction adjacent to protected areas:

The land must remain in forest use after the harvest of the existing timber crop.

Harvesting operations must not impair the ability of the forest to maintain or re-establish a "near-natural" structure and species composition.

Harvesting operations must not impair the soil and water conservation functions of the forest.

Indigenous communities living in the forests should not be deprived of their traditional access to a reasonable harvest of forest products.

Harvesting methods must ensure that adequate regeneration is induced or adequately released if present. This enhances the value of the forest and hence the compulsion to protect it against agricultural encroachment.

Source: Ralph Schmidt, FAO

CASE STUDY 18

The impact of logging on forest adjacent to the Rio Tefe Forest Reserve, Amazonas, Brazil

A study was carried out in 1985 to examine the use by vertebrate species of selectively-logged forest along the edge of the primary forest reserve at Rio Tefe, Brazil. Logging had been carelessly carried out 11 years previously; only 3-5 trees were extracted per hectare, but 60% of trees were destroyed.

Of 12 primate species occurring at the site, two spider monkeys *Ateles* and woolly monkeys *Lagothrix*, were almost entirely restricted to the primary forest areas, making only short forays into logged forest. All the smaller monkeys (tamarins *Saguinus*, squirrel monkeys *Saimiri*, titi monkeys *Callicebus*, and saki monkeys *Pithecia*) are well adapted to edge or naturally-disturbed vegetation types and were more common in the logged than in the unlogged areas. To preserve the more specialised monkeys, such as the spider and woolly monkeys, large areas of primary forest would be required. Groups occupy ranges of up to 6km², therefore blocks of a minimum size of 500km² would be necessary to support viable populations.

The avifauna of the 11-year-old logged forest was quite similar to that of the primary forest. Since a canopy (mostly of *Cecropia*) had re-established microclimatic conditions close to those of the primary forest, even intolerant species such as antbirds (Formicariidae) and foliage-gleaners (Furnariidae) were observed using the logged forest. Mixed-species foraging flocks may well range extensively between both primary and logged forest.

Evidence from elsewhere in Amazonia suggests that recently-logged forest may be temporarily colonised by non-forest species. Provided that primary forest refuges, or areas of old logged forest, remain in proximity to recently-logged blocks, these species are replaced as the forest community develops. However, in isolated logged forests, or in small primary forest "islands" suffering faunal decline, non-forest species tend to persist. To preserve the natural fauna in such cases, large blocks of primary forest would be preferable, but a mosaic of primary and logged forest would suffice if the former is impractical. This has been recommended, for example, in a recent report on the Rio Tefe Forest Reserve.

Source: Andrew Johns, Wildlife Conservation International, Uganda.

BOX 5

The effects of logging on wildlife

Evidence from studies in several regions of the tropics suggests that any level of forest damage during logging may result in the loss of species. In particular, the selective removal of large trees of certain taxa will eliminate their specialised canopy insects and epiphytic plants.

Specialist mammals of timber trees will suffer through logging. Bearded saki monkeys *Chiropotes*, for example, are lost in the eastern Amazon through logging of their food trees which are valuable timbers.

The decomposer fauna and flora of tropical moist forest soils can be seriously affected by microclimatic changes caused by disruption of the canopy. In a study of termites, one of the most important groups of decomposers in tropical environments, the species richness of a selectively logged forest in Sarawak was only half that found in an unlogged forest. In cleared forest the termite fauna was reduced to one quarter of that of the unlogged forest.

Smaller vertebrates are also intolerant of microclimatic changes associated with logging; understorey insectivorous birds may be physiologically stressed in the harsher environment of secondary forest; and small insectivorous bats may lose suitable roost sites through logging.

Most large mammals, however, are resilient to the effects of logging. Large wide-ranging vertebrates are rarely lost where a mosaic of primary forest and logged areas is created. Browsing-species such as elephants and deer typically congregate within the food-rich, recently logged patches.

Source: Andrew Johns, Wildlife Conservation International, Uganda.

CASE STUDY 19

Logging and wildlife in the Sungai Tekam forestry concession, Pahang, West Malaysia

The Sungai Tekam forestry concession is a 315km² commercial, sustained-yield logging concession which has been the site of various studies. It is not part of a protected area but provides information relevant to buffer zone management. The concession is a typical hill dipterocarp forest, of which between 3% and 5% is not loggable. These patches, located on steep slopes, plateaux or waterlogged areas, act as wildlife refuges. They contain a number of vertebrates, such as babblers (Timaliidae) which are largely lost from recently-logged forest. Populations of such intolerant species are able to move outwards from the small refuges to recolonize older logged forest. Evidence from another site, Pasoh Forest Reserve, Negeri Sembilan, suggest that all species have recolonised within 25 years of logging.

Undisturbed patches at Sungai Tekam are used as concentrated food sources by various frugivorous birds such as hornbills (Bucerotidae) and green pigeons *Treron,* but these birds also range widely over logged areas. They feed on only a few kinds of fruit produced by early-successional trees, but appear able to travel between whatever fruiting canopy trees remain. Most mammals have sufficiently varied diets that they are either able to adjust their foraging to take account of the differing availability of food types, as with monkeys and squirrels, or, as with elephants, tapirs and gaur, they make use of the regenerating undergrowth itself. Gaur are wide-ranging and able to travel between both primary and logged patches; they may retreat to the primary refuges to avoid human disturbance, but are more commonly seen in logged than in primary forest.

Studies are continuing at this site but results so far indicate that few vertebrate species are lost by logging of 18 trees per hectare, causing a total damage level of 51% trees destroyed. Almost all the vertebrates that avoid recently logged areas are retained in the primary forest patches left due to difficult terrain. Whether the 3-5% left unlogged is sufficient to maintain populations in the long-term is unclear. Nevertheless, it is significant that such a large proportion of the vertebrate fauna currently persists in recently-logged forest with very small primary forest refuges.

Source: Andrew Johns, Wildlife Conservation International, Uganda

CASE STUDY 20

Reafforestation with indigenous West African timber species

Obeche *Triplochiton scleroxylon* is one of West Africa's more valuable commercial hardwood species. Although quite widespread it has been heavily logged in natural forests. Obeche has been the object of research projects in Nigeria and Britain initiated in 1971.

The work with obeche has illustrated that problems of irregular production and poor seed viability can be circumvented by vegetative propagation, and that this is a relatively easy process, even in a species originally thought to be difficult to root. Perhaps more important, however, the establishment of rooted cuttings in clonal field trials in Nigeria has demonstrated the enormous intra-specific genetic variation that exists in out-breeding tree species. Insect attack is a serious problem in obeche plantation trials at present, but forestry based on selected clones with high productivity, good timber quality, and insect resistance would overcome many of the obstacles currently limiting reafforestation with indigenous species. The research aims primarily at promoting the use of these species in plantations but genetically improved trees could eventually be used to enrich buffer zone forests or to rehabilitate cleared areas in buffer zones.

The approach developed for obeche could be beneficially applied to a much wider range of species, throughout the tropics, so providing an alternative resource of commercially-important species and taking the pressure off natural forests. At the Institute of Terrestrial Ecology near Edinburgh, UK, several dozen tropical timber tree species are being vegetatively propagated experimentally; these include: *Ceiba pentandra, Cleistopholis glauca, Milicia excelsa, Entandrophragma angolense, Khaya ivorensis, Nauclea diderrichii, Terminalia ivorensis, Terminalia superba* and *Triplochiton scleroxylon.*

Source: Roger Leakey, Institute of Terrestrial Ecology, Edinburgh

NON-WOOD FOREST PRODUCTS FROM BUFFER ZONES

Human societies have always derived a vast range of products from forests. Our modern preoccupation with timber will probably prove to be a transitory aberration within a long-term historical perspective. The harvesting of large size timber in the tropics has only occurred on a significant scale since the introduction of power saws and mechanical logging equipment within the past 40 years. The tropical timber boom occurred at a time when temperate timber resources were scarce. The latter are now expanding rapidly and will increasingly compete with tropical timbers in the future.

Traditional societies made use of an abundance of plant and animal products from tropical forests. The work of foresters, biologists, anthropologists and ethnobotanists has produced an abundant literature on the subject. Many thousands of so-called "minor forest products" have been catalogued. The regulation of the harvests of these products was prominent in the mandates of forest departments in the tropics when they were established in the late 19th and early 20th centuries. But in recent decades the search for accelerated economic development has led governments and aid agencies to favour specialisation in the production of a small number of primary commodities for international markets. A wealth of knowledge of non-timber products still exists amongst rural and forest peoples in the tropics, and some (like rattan) have high cash values, but these products are no longer prominent on the agendas of government agencies responsible for tropical forest lands.

With careful harvesting and management many non-timber products can be cropped sustainably with little damage to the biological diversity or ecological functions of buffer zones. They can meet the needs of local communities for food, fibres, medicines, dyes, decorations and recreation. Many of these products can be marketed and thus provide rural people with cash incomes without the need to clear forest land. Many commonplace products in our pharmacies and supermarkets have been developed on the basis of traditional uses and knowledge in the forests of the tropics, and there can be little doubt that many further discoveries remain to be made. And even where such natural products cannot compete with their synthetic or mass-produced equivalents, there is a strong case for preserving the

knowledge and culture associated with their use. Forested buffer zones around protected areas are the obvious place to concentrate efforts towards understanding and rationalising the use of these non-timber products.

Non-timber products can generate revenues to justify retention of tropical forests. But there are many problems associated with any great expansion of their use. Supplies tend to be intermittent, quality is variable, crops are of low volumes and it is difficult to achieve economies of scale, and transport is often a problem. Even when these problems can be overcome there may be little demand in markets which are already attuned to the uniform products of modern industry. A family may be able to earn a living selling fruits from a single hectare of forest near a city in Amazonia; but this does not mean that fruit production from natural forests can pay for the conservation of all the forests of Brazil.

Nonetheless there is much that can be done in buffer zones to realise the benefits of non-timber products. The documentation and monitoring of traditional uses is an essential first step. Measures must be applied to ensure that harvests do not exceed sustainable levels. It is particularly important to regulate access to the resources to authorised individuals or communities. Distinctions have to be made between harvesting for subsistence use and commercial exploitation for distant markets; it may be easier to regulate harvest levels by controlling transport of the crop to distant markets than to attempt to restrict collection within the forest. Preventing villagers from hunting wildlife in forest areas is notoriously difficult, but controlling transport of meat along roads, railways and rivers is much easier.

Care must be taken to avoid promoting a too rapid expansion of the use of non-timber products. Traditional resin-tapping from the pine trees of upland Laos was sustainable as long as the product had to be transported on mules to distant and dispersed markets. Government sponsored industrial refinement and marketing stimulated increased harvesting which killed many of the trees. Industrial scale harvesting of some medicinal plants in the forests of Cameroon has seriously depleted the populations of these plants in the wild. The regeneration of some trees in Amazonia has been impaired by over-harvesting of their fruits. And the felling of palms to harvest the "palm hearts" for consumption in salads is decimating populations of several palm species in different parts of the tropics.

Guidelines

40 Research programmes should document existing uses and economic importance of non-forest products in buffer zones and develop techniques for monitoring the impact of harvesting on the forest ecosystem.

41 Traditional use of non-timber products may be sustainable but care should be taken in promoting increased harvesting as many products may prove susceptible to over-exploitation. Harvest regulations should distinguish between cropping for local use and commercial exploitation for distant markets. The former should be favoured.

42 Any measures to develop new commercial outlets for non-timber products should be associated with careful regulation of harvesting and monitoring of its impact on the resource.

43 It is almost always easier to regulate collection by controls on transport and marketing rather than by direct measures in the forest. This applies particularly to the regulation of hunting.

44 Measures to manage the resource for increased yield can often be associated with the development of new commercial outlets. Propagation of rattan seedlings or cuttings and imposition of close seasons when game populations are breeding are simple resource management measures which can greatly increase yields and their sustainability.

45 Community institutions are rarely strong enough to regulate use of forest products. If ownership is not in private hands it will usually be necessary for restrictions to be enforced by wardens or rangers employed by an appropriate government agency.

Further Reading

Caldecott, J. 1988. Hunting and wildlife management in Sarawak. IUCN Tropical Forest Programme, Gland, Switzerland and Cambridge, UK.

De Beere, J. and McDermott, M. 1989. Economic value of non-timber forest products in South-east Asia. IUCN Netherlands.

Gillis, M. 1986. *Non-wood Forest Products in Indonesia*. Department of Forestry, University of North Carolina, USA.

Peters, C.M., Gentry, A.H. and Mendelsohn, R.O. 1989. Valuation of an Amazonian rainforest. *Nature* 339, pp 655-656.

Sale, J.B. 1981. *The Importance and Values of Wild Plants and Animals in Africa.* IUCN, Gland, Switzerland.

In addition, several titles in the series of FAO Forestry Papers deal with non-wood products. Of special interest are: 34: Fruit-bearing trees (1982), 44: 1, 2, Food and fruit-bearing forest species (1983/84); 67: Some medicinal forest plants of Africa and Latin America (1986). These publications are available in English, French and Spanish from FAO, Rome.

CASE STUDY 21

Harvesting scrubfowl eggs in the Pokili Wildlife Management Area in Papua New Guinea

Pokili is situated on the north coast of West New Britain Province of Papua New Guinea. The Wildlife Management Area covers 112.6km^2 of lowland and swamp forest dominated by the 800m-high volcano, Mount Pago. There is geothermal activity associated with the volcano and the area contains several geysers, hot springs and bubbling mud craters. The nine hectares known as the Pokili Grounds lies around one such geothermal area. Here, using heat from the geothermal source for incubation, the common scrubfowl *Megapodius freycinet* lays its eggs in the ground. This megapode is a dark grey chicken-sized bird with a short tail and large feet. Breeding takes place between April and December when megapodes from the surrounding forest congregate in the communal nesting site. Once the eggs have been laid the adults do not incubate or care for the young. Chicks hatch from the buried eggs, burrow through the earth to the surface and look after themselves until adulthood. Traditionally, landowners have harvested the megapode eggs for food, and more recently for sale.

The Fauna (Protection and Control) Act of 1966 allows customary landowners to have Wildlife Management Areas (WMAs) designated on their land. Rules are established by staff of the Department of Environment and Conservation in consultation with the landowners. A committee selected by the customary landowners is responsible for enforcement of the rules. The Pokili committee is composed of representatives of each of the nine villages who traditionally exploit the megapode eggs. Only land owners can collect eggs, hunting in the area is restricted, and a close season on egg collection is enforced in August. Trees may not be cut, dogs are excluded from the area and soil must be replaced in the holes when eggs are harvested. Committee members and village elders can fine people for killing chicks or adults, failing to replace soil in nesting holes and other offences. But families are reluctant to limit the number of eggs that they harvest and it has proved difficult to prevent non-landowners from poaching eggs from the area. Eggs are now more difficult to find than they were in the past.

Villagers are favourable towards the WMA and value it as a source of income. They do not generally recognise the need to protect the megapode's non-breeding habitat outside the WMA. Everybody recognises that the enforcement of the rules by local people is ineffective. Committee members are not present on each harvest day and they find it hard to penalise friends and relatives.

The general conclusion after 14 years of operation of the scheme is that the concept is good but that control should not lie only in the hands of the local community but with a ranger or warden employed by the provincial government.

Source: King, Betsy. 1990. Does wildlife management by the people work? *Tigerpaper* **17**(1):1-7.

CASE STUDY 22

Forest product utilisation in Sarawak

The indigenous people of the interior of Sarawak are still largely dependent on shifting cultivation, the nature of which varies according to the particular ethnic group involved. Hill rice is the main cultivated crop though, in addition, some groups grow irrigated rice.

Patchworks of cultivation tend to follow the river valleys. In between these are forest areas, often showing no sign of agricultural disturbance. The shifting cultivators and farmers in the longhouse communities of the valleys and nearby slopes depend on the intact moist forest hinterland to a startling degree, for a range of wild species. Recent studies have estimated that wild animal meat contributes almost 150g per person per day. The single most important prey species is the bearded pig *Sus barbatus*, a species of the undisturbed forest.

Riverine fish represent another important subsistence resource; fish stocks are influenced by water quality and this is largely dependent on intact forest. Other forest products harvested primarily for longhouse use include canes or rattans, from which mats, baskets and numerous other items are made; belian *Eusideroxylon zwageri*, an ultra-hard wood used for special construction and roofing; edible fruits, herbs and palm-hearts; and the various feathers, skins, antlers and tusks used for decorative or ritual purposes.

Surplus fish, wild meats and other products are traded for cash in many areas, and gathered mainly for this purpose in some. Engkabang or illipe nuts (oil-rich seeds of the family Dipterocarpaceae); damar or dipterocarp resin; gaharu or incense wood; rattan for processing into marketable goods; and a range of other resins, gums and fruits are harvested from the forest specifically to be sold. Engkabang varies greatly in availability from year to year, but good harvests make for substantial cash earnings. These allow the purchase of goods such as generators, outboard motors and chainsaws. Damar and gaharu are locally more predictable in supply and are often the primary source of cash for a community.

The legal regulation of hunting and gathering rights is a central theme of wildlife resource management in Sarawak. The National Parks Ordinance 1986 makes provision for this by allowing for special rights to hunt and gather to be granted to particular communities when a park is declared. Identified groups of Penan people have, for example, been given the right to continue hunting and gathering in sectors of the Gunung Mulu National Park.

National Parks are one of two kinds of totally protected area in Sarawak, the other being Wildlife Sanctuaries as constituted under the Wildlife Protection Ordinance 1958. A new approach to land use by indigenous people within a protected area is currently being developed for the Lanjak-Entimau Wildlife Sanctuary which was gazetted in 1983. Buffer zones are proposed for the inhabited river valleys which run between the arms of the starfish-shaped sanctuary. These areas will now be brought within the boundaries of the sanctuary but exclusive farming, hunting and gathering rights for the local Iban communities will be retained.

Sources: Julian Caldecott and Francis Gombek, Forest Department, Kuching, Sarawak.
Caldecott, H.J. 1988. Hunting and wildlife management in Sarawak. IUCN Tropical Forest Programme, IUCN, Gland, Switzerland and Cambridge, UK.

CASE STUDY 23

Important forest plant products harvested in the Sinharaja Biosphere Reserve, Sri Lanka

Caryota urens (Palmae), known locally as "kitul", is confined to South India and Sri Lanka. It is a rare understorey tree found in moist forests. The young inflorescence is tapped for its sugary phloem sap which is either fermented, to obtain an alcoholic drink known as "Toddy", or concentrated to prepare a crystalline sugar candy known as "Jaggery". Kitul tapping is a well-established cottage industry in some parts of the country and the traditional methods used are often handed down from generation to generation. Jaggery is a popular sugar substitute and is a readily marketable product, particularly at times when the price of sugar is high. However, no concerted effort has so far been made to bring *Caryota urens* into domestication. Many centuries of tapping of wild plants is thought to be the cause of current rarity.

Rattans and canes of the genus *Calamus*, (Palmae), known locally as "wewal" are much sought after by the villagers for the manufacture of a variety of products. Cane thrives best under partially disturbed forest conditions, in which it often reaches the canopy of the tallest trees. At present, the Forest Department is engaged in propagation and cultivation of cane for plantation in disturbed forest sites and in forest plantations.

Blettaria ensal (Zingiberaceae), known as wild cardamom, is indigenous to South India and Sri Lanka. It is a plant commonly found in the understorey of primary forest. The seeds are harvested as a source of the condiment and, during the fruit ripening period from August to September, large groups of villagers search the forests for this product.

Coscinium fenestrahum (Menispermaceae) is a widespread vine of forest edges, thickets and gaps. The woody stems contain berberine, which is one of the commonest indigenous medicinal Ingredients found in rural, as well as urban households. It is usually taken in combination with other medicinal plant products for the treatment of a variety of ailments, from fever to tetanus. Exploitation is on a substantial scale, threatening the species with extinction. The species is not yet cultivated.

Shorea species (Dipterocarpaceae), the common canopy trees often logged for their medium density timber, also provide a source of food from their rather infrequent mast fruiting. The seeds are traditionally collected and cooked as a vegetable by villagers. Another minor product obtained from some *Shorea* species is resin, which is used in the preparation of varnish and incense.

Vateria copaifera (Dipterocarpaceae) is a sub-canopy tree, endemic to Sri Lanka, and usually found in isolated stands along stream banks. The large seed is pulped and used as a gruel. The bark is used for arresting fermentation of the phloem sap of *Caryota* during the preparation of the sugar candy.

Sources: I.A.U.N. Gunatilleke and C.V.S. Gunatilleke, University of Peridenya, Sri Lanka.

CASE STUDY 24

Medicinal plants of Gunung Leuser National Park, Indonesia

Gunung Leuser National Park covers 8,000km² of tropical moist forest and is probably the most species-rich of all Indonesia's national parks. The park consists of two major mountain ranges, the Leuser-Mamas range to the west and the Kappi-Aras range to the east; they are separated by the heavily-populated Alas-Ranun rift valley, which bisects the park from north to south. The best areas of species-rich lowland forest within the park occur in the Alas valley.

When the park was established in 1980, two populated enclaves were allowed to remain within its boundaries. People who had previously been living elsewhere within the park were translocated into these enclaves. The two settlements Marpunga and Gumpang are both situated in the Alas valley and are surrounded by lowland forest.

Marpunga has a population of about 1,700 people, of Gayo and Alas origin, and Gumpang has 2,500 people, nearly all of whom are Gayo. The economy of the villages is based entirely on agriculture. The valley bottom is used for wet rice cultivation and the lower slopes produce a wide range of crops in gardens known as "kebuns". Forest products are still a source of income for many families,

73

although they are now of declining importance. Over the years, there has been a gradual shift from subsistence to a market economy.

This was accelerated by the completion of a through-road, connecting the villages with the market towns of Kutacane and Blankejeren.

The people of Marpunga and Gumpang have virtually no access to modern medicine and rely almost entirely on medicinal plants administered by native doctors, called "dukuns". It is generally believed that most illnesses are caused by evil spirits which can be overcome by the good spirits contained in plants. A recent study has recorded 171 different plants, including both indigenous and introduced species used in traditional medicine in the villages; 15 species are used in remedies for malaria alone. Some have widespread medicinal application throughout Southeast Asia and are worthy of pharmaceutical investigation. Of the indigenous species some are still collected exclusively from the forest. For example, konyel bark from a *Ficus* species is claimed to be effective against abdominal pain and diarrhoea. Others are both cultivated and gathered from the wild. One of these is the red sugar palm *Arenga pinnata*, which is used mainly to sweeten unpalatable medicinal preparations, but may have curative properties in its own right and is added to a wide range of remedies. Medicinal plants provide a source of income for the villagers and are collected for sale on traditional medicine stalls in the markets of Kutacane and Blankejeren.

Source: Elliott, S. and Brimacombe, J. 1985. The medicinal plants of Gunung Leuser National Park, Indonesia. WWF Report.

CASE STUDY 25

Butterflies pay for research in Belize

Shipstern Reserve is a 9,600ha forest reserve in northern Belize, situated on the coast near the border with Mexico. Sustainable use of the tropical forest is a major objective of the reserve, with the aim that it will become financially self-supporting. The first product to be harvested sustainably is live butterflies. Butterfly breeding facilities being set up on the reserve include ten netted enclosures covering about one hectare of land, and gardens to produce food plants. Live pupae will be produced for the export market - mainly to the increasingly popular butterfly houses in Britain.

Butterfly houses are heated greenhouses where tropical butterflies are displayed for the education and amusement of paying visitors. The industry in Britain has a turnover in excess of US $8 million a year from about 50 establishments, using half a million butterfly pupae a year. Interest is spreading rapidly to other European countries. The main suppliers of pupae are in Malaysia, the Philippines, India, Taiwan and the USA, but growth is expected in Central America, Indonesia and possibly Africa. Butterfly breeding is clearly an economic operation which can help in species conservation, provide funds for conservation programmes and create jobs associated with tropical forest protected areas.

Marketing of captive-bred butterfly pupae from Shipstern will be a major source of funding for further development of the reserve's facilities. A visitor centre and research centre are planned. Research will concentrate on multi-disciplinary studies of ecology, local land-use and the development of mariculture techniques appropriate for local conditions.

BOX 6

Rattan Cultivation

In Southeast Asia, climbing palms, or rattans, are commercially the second most important forest product after timber. Their main commercial use is in furniture production, though they are extremely versatile with a wide range of traditional uses.

Rattans occur naturally in the tropical forests of Southeast Asia; a few species are also found in West African forests. Virtually all the rattans in trade are collected from the wild. Increasing demand for canes, together with high rates of logging, are leading to useful species becoming more and more scarce. In Indonesia, for example, many forest areas near rural settlements have been overcut, leaving almost no commercial rattans. Indonesia, the Philippines and Thailand now ban the export of raw canes; and the export of semi-processed and processed canes from Peninsular Malaysia is prohibited, so as to sustain the supply for domestic industry. In general, there is a trend to process raw rattan into manufactured goods within the producer countries to generate increased incomes, higher revenue earnings and create employment.

Box 6, contd ...

Rattan collection, cultivation and processing provide important possibilities for buffer zone schemes around protected areas. Planting indigenous species can help to rehabilitate logged forest and justify the maintenance of forest cover. Already, rattan plantations are being established in the Sinharaja Biosphere Reserve, Sri Lanka (Case Study 31) and are planned for Dumoga Bone National Park, Sulawesi.

Propagation and cultivation of most rattan species are still at the experimental stage. The two main species grown commercially are the small-diameter rattans *Calamus trachycoleus* ("rotan irit") and *Calamus caesius* ("rotan sega"), used for weaving, binding and mat-making. The largest area of cultivation for these species is in Central Kalimantan Province where a plantation was established over a hundred years ago. Other species should also be considered for buffer zones, to supply local needs, expand trade and as a conservation measure.

The usual method of propagation for rattans is to raise plants from seed. Fruits of nearly all rattans contain only one seed and direct sowing usually leads to heavy losses of seed and newly germinated plants. It is more efficient to plant out seedlings, raised in nurseries, which have been protected from predation and the direct effects of weather. Naturally-occurring rattans within protected areas and buffer zones should be protected as 'seed orchards', to conserve seed for planting. Mother plants to provide seed are generally located in increasingly remote and inaccessible forest areas. Indigenous people often know where to find the ripe fruits and are skilled in harvesting them from the forest canopy. Rattan schemes in buffer zones should draw on such local skills.

The collection of rattans to meet basic local needs should be allowed in buffer zones. Rattans can be very important in traditional cultures and in India, for example, some species have immense ethnobotanical value. They are particularly important to tribal people in remote areas of the country, providing medicines, material for bows and arrows, thatching, bridge construction, cordage and draglines for fishing, and as a source of soft drinking water.

Manufacture of traditional rattan products should be encouraged in buffer zones where there is a sustainable supply of the raw material. Basketware and matting using traditional designs could, for example, be an appropriate form of rattan use. In Malaysia the Accelerated Village Industry Development Programme is promoting the development and marketing of high-quality rattan handicrafts through village co-operatives. Information on rattans can be obtained from the Rattan Information Centre, Forest Research Institute, Kepong, Malaysia.

Source: Wong, K.M. & Manokaran, N. (Eds.) Rattan: report of a meeting held in Kuala Lumpur, October 1984.

CASE STUDY 26

Mango conservation in the Kutai National Park, Kalimantan, Indonesia

Kalimantan is the centre of origin for a number of important tropical fruit trees, including species of mango *Mangifera*, durian *Durio* and breadfruit *Artocarpus*. A recent study has shown that of 16 species of mango which occur in East Kalimantan Province, 13 are edible. Individual mango trees are widely scattered throughout the forest, and the conservation of species in the wild requires large undisturbed areas. Several species have been recorded in Kutai National Park.

Conservation of wild mangoes within protected areas can only form part of a programme to preserve the full diversity of edible forms. Most of the edible species have been brought into semi-cultivation and are grown in the ladangs or surrounding secondary forest near to settlements. The semi-cultivated species and primitive cultivars, together with wild relatives of cultivated species, represent a unique gene-pool which is closely linked to traditional life-styles. Local Dayak people are a rich source of knowledge on the genetic variety of mangoes and the conservation of the breeding potential of the fruit is dependent on the wise use of this knowledge.

Traditionally, shifting cultivators in Kalimantan did not cut down fruit trees or other useful species when clearing the forest for agriculture. Other groups, such as the Punan nomadic hunter-gatherers, planted wild fruit trees along their migration routes, both for food and to attract wild animals. The sedentary groups of Dayaks, settled along rivers, still set up temporary encampments in the forest during the fruit season to collect wild mangoes and other fruits. Sadly local knowledge of the wild fruit resources is being lost as life-styles change; at the same time, increasing pressures on the forest lead to the loss of valuable fruit trees. Newcomers to Kalimantan, such as the settlers from Java, have no knowledge of the different mango species.

Buffer zone schemes, with their emphasis on meeting local needs, provide ideal opportunities for the conservation of semi-cultivated plant resources and land races which will compliment the conservation of truly wild species in strictly protected natural reserves.

Source: Bompard, J.M. and Kostermans, A.J.G.H. Preliminary results of an IUCN/WWF sponsored project for conservation of wild *Mangifera* species *in situ* in Kalimantan.

CASE STUDY 27

Harvesting giant snails in the Taï Forest, Côte D'Ivoire

The Dutch-sponsored *Tropenbos* programme is proposing to conduct research on the possibility of sustained yield management of populations of the African giant snail *Achatina achatina* in the buffer zone around the Taï National Park in Côte d'Ivoire. These snails provide a protein rich food which is highly appreciated by the local population. Demand is already high, it is estimated that 8,000 tonnes were sold in 1986. The snails are easy to catch, can be kept alive for up to a week, and come ready packed for transport in their own shells. Each snail provides between 100g and 300g of meat, with no waste. The snails produce up to 200 eggs per year and grow rapidly. They are forest dwellers and commercial use of the snails would provide an argument for conserving natural forest in the buffer zone. The fact that they are not game animals means that more intensive management would not require any complicated legal changes. Lastly, the shells are a valuable source of calcium for animal feed or crop fertilization.

Source: Vooren, A. P. (In press) Appropriate buffer zone management strategies for the Taï National Park, Côte d'Ovoire in *Actes de l'Atelier sur l'aménagement et la conservation de l'ecosystem forestier tropical humide*. Cayenne, Guyane Française, Mars 1990, MAB-Unesco, Paris, France.

CASE STUDY 28

Iguanas and ornamental plants in the Talamanca Region, Costa Rica

Pilot programmes supported by the local NGO, ANAI (Case Studies 3 and 14), are helping to create new sources of income and new food supplies for forest dwelling communities in the Talamanca region of southeastern Costa Rica. The flesh of the indigenous green iguana is an important food of native people. Over-exploitation was leading to a reduction of wild populations and a risk of local extinction in some areas. It has been found that the animals breed and grow well in captivity. Females produce over 30 eggs per year and the iguanas feed on the foliage of forest tree species and thus do not compete with conventional livestock. It has also been found that the iguanas will remain in areas where they are released into the wild. Captive stocks are now being build-up and it is planned to make breeding stock available to local people in order to repopulated forests around their villages.

Costa Rica is an important exporter of ornamental plants. Many of the *Araceae* and *Marantaceae* palms which grow in the deep shade of the forest are well adapted to decorate the warm shady houses of people in the industrialised world. Most of the export trade is met by plants grown in huge shaded nurseries. Botanists in Talamanca are now looking for new species which could be grown in bulk for export. The palm genus *Reinhardtia* appears to be particularly suitable for this purpose and is now being grown on a small scale.

The possibility is now being investigated of propagating some of these ornamental species in areas where the ground vegetation has been cleared under the forest canopy. Indian communities would then be able to engage in an income generating activity whilst retaining forest cover near their homes.

Already many forest communities gather medicinal plants and sell them on local markets. Ways of managing these plant resources for increased yield and of improving marketing possibilities are being investigated.

Sources: Asociacion ANAI, San Jose, Costa Rica.
Rafael Ocampo and Alejandro Imbach, Centro Agronomico Tropical de Investigacion y Ensenanza (CATIE), Turrialba, Costa Rica.

CASE STUDY 29

Non-wood forest products from the Maya Biosphere Reserve in the Peten region of Guatemala

The Peten region of present day Guatemala was the centre of the classical Mayan empire in the 9th to 12th Centuries A.D. For unknown reasons the Maya abandoned the area in the 12th Century and it remained largely uninhabited until the end of the 19th Century. A modest local economy then developed based on the harvesting of mahogany *Swietinia*, cedar *Cedrela* and "chicle" (the resin of *Manilkara zapota*) for the manufacture of chewing gum. Subsequently, all-spice *Pimenta dioica* began to be exploited as a condiment. All of these trees were natives of the Peten forests.

When synthetic chewing gum displaced chicle from much of its traditional market, many local people switched to collecting and exporting "xate", the fronds of two species of *Chamaedorea* palms, for wreath-making in the USA and Europe. At present more than 7,000 families earn a living from the extraction of chicle, allspice and xate from the Peten. The forest has remained in a near-natural state and retained much of its conservation value.

Population increase and competition for land in the south of Guatemala is forcing many people to move north and clear the forested areas of the country for agriculture. The "agricultural frontier" is now entering the Peten forests and posing a threat both to the conservation values of the area and to the welfare of the local Indian populations.

The one million hectare Maya biosphere reserve was established in early 1990 to protect the natural resources and traditional way of life of the people. Much of the area will be managed as a buffer zone for several totally protected areas in the Peten. Various intensities of use will be permitted in these buffer zones. They will range from improvements in the resource security and marketing infrastructure for chicle, all-spice and xate gatherers, through selective forest management for high value timbers to intensive use of some good agricultural lands for food production.

The natural forests and architectural ruins in the area are major tourist attractions and tourism is expected to contribute significantly to the local economy.

Source: Alejandro Imbach and the staff of the Centro Agronomico Tropical de Investigacion y Ensenanza, Turrialba, Costa Rica.

7 RESEARCH, EDUCATION AND TOURISM IN BUFFER ZONES

Protected areas, almost by definition, are locations with outstanding natural features or with extensive tracts of natural vegetation. They are focal points for recreational visits and are prime sites for many kinds of research on the natural environment. In many countries the economic advantages to be gained from tourism are a major factor in establishing parks and reserves. In addition, numerous protected areas have been established to protect locations whose special scientific value was originally demonstrated by research programmes.

In many countries, especially the poorer ones, it would be difficult to stimulate any popular support for protected area programmes if it were not for their economic value for tourism. Protected area authorities are sometimes located in ministries of tourism or commerce. In both industrialised and developing countries, tourism and research are generally actively promoted in protected area systems.

The main focus of research, education and tourism is normally the strictly protected core zone or conservation area of a national park or reserve. But when these activities generate high intensities of use, or when they require manipulation or modification of the habitat, it may be better to locate them in buffer zones. Tourism and research all contribute to protected area conservation programmes by creating employment for local people, providing markets for local products and thus cash for local economies. They also raise national and international awareness of the interest and value of a site. Research programmes also contribute to the understanding of the ecological and social issues that influence conservation programmes.

The nature and degree of benefits that accrue to a protected area vary greatly according to the ways in which the tourist and research activities are organised. The economic benefits can easily go to tour operators in distant cities and by-pass the local communities. Land speculation and monopolies on facilities can allow a few people to get rich whilst impoverishing others. The infrastructure and economic activity associated with tourism can bring excessive development to ecologically fragile areas and visitors can themselves damage the environment by polluting waters, dumping garbage, cutting firewood, collecting unusual plants and animals, and by the impact of their numbers, noise and the physical facilities that they require.

Research is generally a positive influence on protected areas. Researchers are usually aware of their environment and the problems of its conservation. They often spend long periods in the field and develop an understanding and knowledge of local peoples and their problems. They are often the first to notice, and draw attention to, emerging conservation issues. Through their interactions with protected area staff and visitors they raise awareness of the values of the areas where they work. And by taking their knowledge and interest back to their universities they introduce the concepts of conservation to future generations of students.

Midway between tourism and research lies the rapidly expanding area of specialised natural history tourism. Increasing numbers of amateur naturalists now devote their leisure time to the study of the birds, mammals, plants and general environmental issues of natural areas. Many of these people have a relatively sophisticated knowledge of the fauna and flora of protected areas and their conservation problems. They are often members of conservation organisations and many make voluntary financial contributions to conservation programmes.

Interest in tourism in tropical forests is now so great that fees paid by visitors are sufficient to pay for conservation programmes. This has led to the development of private reserves in some of the more attractive and accessible areas of the tropics. A recent study by WWF-US showed that the standards of management of these private reserves was often higher than that of government managed reserves. It also showed that the private owners often developed more effective buffer zone activities than their governmental counterparts. Countries such as Costa Rica and Ecuador have highly developed tourism industries based on tropical forest protected areas and in both countries the private sector has made valuable contributions to conservation. In Costa Rica protected area legislation is now being reviewed to determine whether it needs to be modified to better address the needs of the rapidly expanding network of private conservation areas.

Guidelines

46 Excessive or poorly controlled tourism can damage the resources of protected areas, but on balance the interest and income generated by tourism make valuable contributions to conservation programmes.

47 Many of the physical facilities required for tourism and research can be located in buffer zones, outside of the totally protected area. Car parks, accommodation, camping and picnic areas, information centres and other facilities should all normally be located in buffer zones. The quality of the experience of visitors will be improved if these facilities are located in near-natural environments: a good incentive for maintaining natural vegetation in buffer zones.

48 The nature and location of tourist developments in buffer zones must be strictly controlled. Centres of development should not be too close to the protected area boundary or to ecologically sensitive sites.

49 The private sector should be encouraged to manage intensive-use conservation areas in buffer zones. These can provide an attractive physical environment for accommodation facilities and can reduce pressure on strictly protected core zones or conservation areas.

50 Legal and planning measures should be sought to control tourist development. Access routes for tourism must not be available to poachers, loggers and other illegal resource users. Strict controls must be imposed upon waste disposal. Special measures may be required to reduce the risk of visitors setting fires.

51 Tourist development should not be allowed to encourage or facilitate settlement in buffer zones. Existing local residents should have preference in employment and service activities generated by tourism. (In reality it has usually proved difficult to avoid domination of tourist development by outside commercial interests).

52 Measures to limit incidental tourist activities are often necessary. Sports and other intensive recreational activities which are not related to the special interest of the natural area should not be developed in the buffer zone. Discothèques, golf courses and tennis courts, for example, are inappropriate for buffer zones and should be located as far as possible from the protected area.

53   In ecologically or culturally sensitive areas, the interests of conservation may be better met by low-volume, high-price tourism rather than by mass low-price tourism. This is especially true in areas where large numbers of tourists might have a disruptive impact on indigenous communities.

54   Tourism must be controlled and monitored, both in the protected area and in the buffer zone. Collection of plants and animals must be prevented, trampling of sensitive vegetation avoided by restricting visitors to paths, and disturbance of wildlife kept to a minimum.

55   The provision of appropriate documentation and signposting can do much to improve the quality of the visitors' experience and influence them towards activities and behaviour which will diminish their impact on the resources of the area. It will also contribute to raising their general environmental awareness.

56   Research which requires collecting plants and animals or any manipulation of the environment, should, as far as possible, be restricted to areas of near-natural vegetation in buffer zones. Special research areas may need to be established for this purpose, from which casual visitors are excluded.

57   Use of protected areas by groups of students for environmental education purposes should in general be encouraged. The intensity of such use may be such that it is preferable to concentrate it in buffer zones rather than in the strictly protected core zone or conservation area.

58   The results of research carried out in and around protected areas should be freely available to management staff and other researchers in the same area. This may require the establishment of a documentation centre. Foreign researchers must be obliged to deposit copies of research reports with the protected area authority.

Further Reading

Boo, E. 1990. *Ecotourism: The Potentials and Pitfalls.* WWF-US.
McNeely, J.A. and Thorsell, J.W. (In press) Guidelines for development of terrestrial and marine national parks for tourism and travel. World Tourist Organisation, Madrid, Spain.

CASE STUDY 30

The Monteverde Cloud Forest, Costa Rica

Monteverde is a private nature reserve of 10,000ha, located between 800m and 1,860m above sea level, in the Tilaran mountains of northern Costa Rica. The reserve is owned and managed by the Tropical Science Centre, a non-profit Costa Rican association. In 1987 almost 13,000 people visited the reserve and the number is growing each year. Visitors stay in a number of small hotels in mixed forest and agricultural land lying below the reserve boundary to the south. The number of hotels is increasing rapidly and associated facilities, such as souvenir shops and restaurants, are being developed.

The expansion of agriculture in the lower Pacific slopes below the reserve was destroying forest and provoking erosion in the areas where tourist facilities were located. These lower lying forests are seasonally important habitats for some of the fauna of the reserve itself. In 1986 some resident local biologists and farmers formed the Monteverde Conservation League with the objective of protecting these lower Pacific slopes as a form of buffer zone for the reserve. They raised money locally from visitors and internationally from conservation organisations in industrialised countries. The value of contributions has been increased by the use of donated funds to purchase discounted Costa Rican government debt - a debt swap.

The league has purchased farmland in the buffer zone and is restoring natural forest cover on it. They are also conducting educational programmes for local children. A guided trail has been established in a mosaic forest/farmland area in the buffer zone and it is much used by tourists. Visitors can observe the impact of past agriculture on the forest and the efforts of the league to restore the habitat. A recent initiative is the "childrens rainforest" campaign. Children in Sweden, Canada, United Kingdom, Japan and Germany are raising money for the purchase of additional land for the reserve. Some of these children are visiting Monteverde to see the forest that they have purchased. It is hoped that this initiative might grow into a loose network of private forest reserves, each adopted by a childrens group, and located throughout the tropics.

The Monteverde Conservation League provides a forum for debate of issues affecting the reserve and its surroundings. There is considerable discussion of the economic impact of tourism. Income to the reserve, mainly from entry fees, now exceeds US$30,000 per year (1987 figure), and a cooperative craft shop selling local handicrafts has sales in excess of US$50,000 per year. Many residents would like tourism to remain small scale and are concerned that the benefits should not be excessively concentrated in the hands of a minority of people. Land prices are escalating and this is constraining traditional activities in the area. A recent focus of the league has been on improving the conservation practices of local farmers.

Source: Jim Crisp, President, Monteverde Conservation League.

CASE STUDY 31

Sinharaja Research Programme, Sri Lanka

Botanical studies are being carried out in the Sinharaja Biosphere Reserve to provide basic information for future programmes of propagation and breeding of indigenous plants and to provide a scientific base for management and conservation of the forest's genetic resources.

- **Population Structure.** Phytosociological surveys are being carried out to describe the population structure of each species, and to measure mortality, from flower bud initiation to seedling establishment; causes of mortality will also be studied where possible.

- **Reproductive Biology.** Pollination biology, mating systems and embryology of plant species are being studied to establish their intrinsic potential for gene exchange under forest conditions, and also their amenability to breeding. This will be useful in selecting variants for domestication under a variety of climatic and soil conditions.

- **Genetic Diversity.** Evidence provided by allozymes, combined with biometric studies, is being used in studies of patterns of genetic variation between and within wild populations.

It is envisaged that the results from this study will: (i) facilitate the exploitation of native plant species in village home gardens or agroforestry systems; (ii) provide estimates of genetic erosion due to current exploitation practices; (iii) identify the principal biological and environmental needs for the survival of the species chosen; and (iv) contribute towards the development of a rational strategy for conservation and management of the species in the wild and in cultivation.

Ecological studies are also being carried out, looking at the contribution of primary production and nutrient cycling to soil fertility in the natural forest, deforested lands and forest plantations. This work includes a survey of mycorrhizal associations, in the various natural and modified forest habitats. Information collected on soil conditions will be useful in planning reforestation.

Source: I.A.U N. Gunatilleke and C.V.S. Gunatilleke, University of Peridenya, Sri Lanka.

CASE STUDY 32

Research and scientific tourism at La Selva Reserve in Costa Rica

La Selva Reserve is an area of moist forest in the Atlantic lowlands of Costa Rica, with a total area of 1,366ha. About 90% of the reserve is undisturbed species-rich forest. There are over 1,800 plant species, 388 birds and 143 butterflies in the reserve together with a wide range of other species. The remaining 10% of La Selva was planted some years ago with cacao, peach palm and laurel. Parts of the disturbed areas have been converted to an arboretum and a rotational series of strips for studying forest.

Research facilities at La Selva include a laboratory completed in 1983. This has air-conditioned work space for 30 researchers, a wide range of field and laboratory equipment, a library and taxonomic reference collections. Accommodation is available for visitors. Access to the forest is facilitated by an extensive system of trails and bridges. Three permanent four-hectare research plots were established in 1970 on the major soil types (residual, swamp and old alluvial). Computerised data are available on all trees 10 centimetres or more in diameter which occur in these plots.

Proposed research projects at La Selva are subject to the approval of the Organization for Tropical Studies, Inc. (OTS) which has offices in Costa Rica and the USA. The conservation importance of La Selva is paramount and researchers are required to submit full details and scientific justification for any proposed collecting. Cooperation with local scientists is encouraged through OTS.

Researchers are given preference for the use of La Selva's facilities but other visitors may stay when space is available. Daily and weekly rates for accommodation, use of laboratory facilities and access to the forest vary according to the purpose of the visit. Preferential rates are offered to Costa Rican students and researchers.

Source: Tropical Science Center, San José, Costa Rica.

CASE STUDY 33

Tourist trekking in Khao Yai National Park, Thailand

The northwest section of Khao Yai National Park, Thailand, is an attractive area for wilderness trekking. It has mountain vistas, scenic rivers, waterfalls and forests with good wildlife populations, sufficient to attract both national and international visitors. The development of tourist trekking is seen as a way to generate income for local villagers in a manner compatible with conservation objectives. Without sufficient income, local people have previously exploited park resources out of economic necessity.

Treks are taken into Khao Yai from the village of Ban Sap Tai. The first day and night are spent in the village, allowing trekkers to experience life in a rural Thai community. The visitors are welcomed by local school teachers who introduce them to the village and briefly explain the trekking programme's objectives. The remaining days are spent hiking and camping in the park.

In promoting the trekking programme emphasis is put on the adventure of exploring tropical moist forest in a scenic and virtually unchanged area of Thailand. The wildlife interest is not promoted strongly since wildlife sightings are relatively infrequent, due to the nature of the forest and secretive habits of the animals. The treks have attracted a wide variety of participants, most of whom have been expatriates residing in Thailand.

The villagers have benefited financially from the programme, with money received for guide and porter services and for transportation. Villagers are, as a result, becoming more sympathetic to conservation, as they appreciate that the national park can provide them with tangible benefits. The trekking programme has considerable potential for expansion but, as yet, is limited by the lack of bilingual trek leaders and inadequate administration. Solutions to these problems are being sought as part of the overall management programme for the national park.

Source: Dobias, R.J. 1985. Elephant conservation and protected area management. WWF/IUCN Project 3001 Final Report.

CASE STUDY 34

Tourism and education values of the Orang-utan Rehabilitation Centre at Gunung Leuser National Park, Sumatra, Indonesia

The Bohorok Rehabilitation Centre for orang-utans *Pongo pygmaeus* is situated just inside the Gunung Leuser National Park. It is one of Sumatra's major tourist attractions and each year receives up to 5,000 domestic and 1,000 foreign visitors. Visitor numbers to the centre itself are controlled, but many more people visit the car park area for picnicking, swimming and camping. Public education is one of the main purposes and activities of the rehabilitation centre.

The closest village to the Bohorok Centre is Bukit Lawang, about 1.5km away. Villagers benefit from tourism through entrance fees to the village, car parking fees, guiding and the provision of accommodation and food. The economic value of the Centre is also appreciated by the provincial tourist service, particularly as the area is within easy reach of the large city of Medan. Tourism developments include improvements to the camping ground and a proposed new education centre.

Unfortunately, forestry interests have been threatening the tourism potential of the Bohorok Centre and surrounding area. An area of state forest close to the centre has been logged for large dipterocarp trees since 1981 and the forested slopes facing the centre are now degraded, with obvious gaps in the canopy and a number of bare mud slides. The Office of Nature Conservation for Northern Sumatra has been offered this land as a tourist forest but restoration of the forest is required.

In the long term, the recreation value of the Bohorok Centre is worth more than logging to the local people. Proceeds from logging have long since dried up for the villagers of Bukit Lawang, whereas tourism provides a sustainable income.

Source: Whitten, A.J. and Ranger, J. 1986. Logging at Bohorok. *Oryx*, **20**(4): 246-248.

8 SELECTED REFERENCES

Annis, S. 1987. Can small-scale development be a large-scale policy? The case of Latin America. *World Development* **15**(Supplement): 129-134.

Batisse, M. 1986. Developing and focusing the biosphere reserve concept. *Nature and Resources* **22**: 1-10.

Boo, E. 1990. *Ecotourism: The Potentials and Pitfalls*. World Wildlife Fund, Washington, DC.

Brown, L.D. and Korten, D.C. 1989. *Understanding Voluntary Organisations: Guidelines for Donors*. Policy, Planning and Research Working Paper 258. The World Bank, Washington, DC.

Bunch, R. 1982. *Two Ears of Corn: A Guide to People-centred Agricultural Improvement*. World Neighbours, Oklahoma.

Carruthers, I. and Chambers, R. 1981. Rapid appraisal for rural development. *Agricultural Administration* **8**(6): 407-422.

Centre for International Development and Environment and the National Environment Secretariat, Government of Kenya. 1990. *Participatory Rural Appraisal Handbook*. Natural Resources Management Support Series No. 1. World Resources Institute, Washington, DC.

Cernea, M. (Ed.) 1985. *Putting People First; Sociological Variables in Rural Development*. Oxford University Press, New York. The World Bank, Washington, DC.

Cernea, M. 1988. *Nongovernmental Organisations and Local Development*. Discussion Paper No. 40. The World Bank, Washington, DC.

Cohen, J.M. and Uphoff, N.T.. 1977. *Rural Development Participation: Concepts and Measures for Project Design, Implementation and Evaluation*. Monograph No. 2, Rural Development Committee, Centre for International Studies, Cornell University, New York.

Commission on National Parks and Protected Areas. 1984. *Threatened Protected Areas of the World*. IUCN, Gland, Switzerland.

Doolette, J.B. and Magrath, W.B. (Eds.) 1990. *Watershed Development in Asia: Strategies and Technologies*. Technical Paper Number 127. The World Bank, Washington, DC.

Gregersen, H.S. Draper and Elz, D. (Eds.) 1989. *People and Trees: The Role of Social Forestry in Sustainable Development*. Economic Development Institute, World Bank, Washington, DC.

Hales, D. 1989. Changing concepts of national parks. *In:* D. Western and M. Pearl (Eds.), *Conservation for the Twenty-first Century*. Oxford University Press, New York.

Hough, J. 1988a. Biosphere reserves: myth and reality. *Endangered Species Update* **6**(1/2): 1-4. School of Natural Resources, University of Michigan, USA.

Hough, J. 1988b. Obstacles to effective management of conflicts between national parks and surrounding communities in developing countries. *Environmental Conservation* **15**(2): 129-136.

Hough, J. and Sherpa, N.T. 1989. Bottom-up versus basic needs: integrating conservation and development in the Annpurna and Michiru Mountain Conservation Areas of Nepal and Malawi. *Ambio* **18**(8): 434-441.